D0732994

Lost Dreams

When the path you are on

is irreversibly altered

To my dear
friend Erin
&
DMBell

Dawn M. Bell

Published by
DBell Publishing, LLC
Winter Park, FL

Printed in the United States of America

Library of Congress Control Number: 2016919306
Bell, Dawn M.

FIRST EDITION

Paperback ISBN: 978-0-9906438-4-5
eBook ISBN: 978-0-9906438-5-2

Scripture references marked RSV are taken from the Revised Standard Version of the Bible. Copyright © 1946, 1952, and 1971 the Division of Christian Education of the National Council of the Churches of Christ in the United States of America. Used by permission. All rights reserved.

Scripture references marked NIV are taken from the New International Version (NIV) Holy Bible, New International Version®, NIV®. Copyright ©1973, 1978, 1984, 2011 by Biblica, Inc.® Used by permission. All rights reserved worldwide.

Jacket art direction and graphic design by: Kymi Swanepoel

Front jacket photo:
Shutterstock image ID#: 164721908 © Eugene Sergeev

Table of Contents

Introduction

by Dawn M. Bell

Almost six years have passed since the loss of my husband, Matthew Bell. It's been two and a half years since I finished writing *Wife of the Deceased*, a memoir taken from my journal entries during the three and a half years following Matt's death.

The catalyst behind writing *Wife of the Deceased* was my frustration with finding a book that could validate my feelings and actions while grieving. I could find no resource that explained and justified the physical, mental, and emotional pain I was suffering. As I healed, I felt compelled to write the book I wish I'd been given when I needed it. My goal was to create a resource for grievers unlike what was available at the time.

Two things surprised me as I wrote and published my debut book. The first was how hard it was to write a book, regardless of the subject. It seems like the enormity of the challenge would have been obvious, but it wasn't. It was an Everest-like feat to pen a book of 60,000+ words when I'd written only a few short stories averaging 1,000 words each, most of them fifteen to twenty years earlier. Not surprisingly it was even harder to weave my journal entries into a story depicting the most painful event in my life. The agony was second only to losing Matt. It forced me to experience the loss again and again.

I feared launching my memoir, because of the transparency with which I wrote. I basically opened up my diary for the world to read, if they so chose. I was nearly paralyzed by fear of the judgment and ridicule that I was sure to follow. I finished the first draft and sent it to an editor thinking that even if I never went through with publishing it, at least I would have a professional copy to print for my daughter and me. During the seven weeks that it took for my manuscript to be edited, I wrestled with whether or not to publish it every hour of every day.

Eventually, I did publish the book. I had it printed in paperback to be sold through Amazon and Barnes & Noble, and I uploaded the e-book version on Kindle and Nook and launched both versions on October 4, 2014.

Next came the second surprise.

My fears were never realized. Readers neither ridiculed nor judged me. Readers embraced me, sometimes literally. They thanked me for my honesty while in turn sharing their own stories of loss. Many told me how my memoir affected them, how it helped them understand the behavior of loved ones who had suffered a loss, or their own actions while grieving, sometimes decades earlier. For months I was gifted with beautiful messages that arrived by phone, Email, text message, and letter.

Whether it was face-to-face or if the reader wrote to me, most people started with, "My loss is nothing like yours, but…" Every time I heard or read this line I cringed. It broke my heart because people were minimizing their own experiences.

All loss is the loss of a dream. The dream is the path people thought their life would take, how they once envisioned their future. The path is irreversibly altered by the loss. While some losses may be deemed less painful, the first loss is ground zero for the sufferer. It's the worst pain that person has ever felt and should in no way be minimized.

This realization was the motivation behind *Lost Dreams.* I wanted to illustrate that dreams are lost in many ways and each will produce its own manner of grief. My aim is to encourage compassion for all types of loss, no matter the measure.

To gather stories, I issued a contest requesting nonfiction portrayals of loss in less than 4,000 words. The winning submissions would be assembled in a book titled *Lost Dreams,* and each winner would receive a copy.

I chose the winning entries solely on content. Author's names or story placement in the book is not indicative of or based on any ranking system.

Please read each story with an equal appreciation for the loss and ensuing grief cycle experienced by each author, regardless of the perceived level of devastation.

It's not easy to share a story of personal loss and pain. I applaud every one of the contest entrants for having the courage to do so.

It is truly my honor to introduce the winning authors:

Jules Zurich   Fred Cliett
Dayna Bodensteiner   Deborah Hope
James Robert Starkey   Donna Parrey
Emily Keese   Fern Goodman

Shellie Ambrose-Harms

Pamela Sullins

John Hope

Diane Payne

Joyce Hess

Beda Kantarjian

Alora Gilman

Arielle Haughee

Stephanie Marinos Boda

Erika Hoffman

Diane McMinn

Mary McKinstray

Joan M. D. Coonprom

Kierra Dann

1

Loss of a Sibling Through No Fault of His Own

by Joyce Hess

Current Age: 65
Age at time of loss: 10-65

In Memory of Danny,
November 28, 1959 – May 31, 2016

We have all lost someone or something; eyesight, hearing, etc. Many things can be lost. The life devastation of loss I am going to share is one many know of; however, many do not speak of it. Why won't we, they, us speak of it? It, the reason, is social stigma. It is the stigma of mental illness.

There are of course many types of loss from mental illness; loss of marriage, loss of family, loss of time, and loss of special occasions. I could go on and on. When you have a family member who has a brain disorder, your whole world turns upside down, in and out, with shattered dreams, missed parties, and lost moments. You lose yourself in the whirlwind of exhaustion, the up-we-go, down-we-go of daily life.

You wake in the morning looking at the sky. "Ahhh, it is blue, puffy white clouds, a cool refreshing breeze that flows over you, and then all of a sudden there it is, looming like a heavy gray ball of black twine all tangled up so horribly there is no way to untangle it. You remember, "Oh, that's right. He is in crisis. I need to call the case manager. I need to get the crisis team together." What can we do? What can we do today to help him try to become part of this earth again?

Damn it, I will have to miss art class again. Sorry dear, we need to cancel the trip to the coast. He is in crisis. I must help him. Lost holidays. Lost movies, lost barbeques, but then I stop to realize what he has lost.

He lost it all, including his girlfriend. He has no children to love. No college. One thing he did find was jail. Jail with no compassion for his illness. He was locked in a cell with no proper medicine to keep the demons at bay. He lost his dream to be a drummer in a rock band. He lost his dream for the life he fights so hard for every day, every minute to keep on track. Okay, we will let you have the housing again. You can come three times a week to the mental health office to receive your medicine and your money for the week and to check with your case manager. "How did you do this week? What is your plan for the upcoming week?"

"I thought I would try to get the dishes washed and get a voucher for some new shoes. Dad will take me grocery shopping. We do that together. He is a bargain hunter. I don't manage my money very well alone."

"Okay, I will see you next week so we can do this all over again."

Concerts not attended too often; movies, sometimes. There are too many people and voices. When you are mentally ill you don't fit in many places, because you are scared, nervous that the anxiety might show through. Others might find out. You lose your thoughts fast. You feel paranoid to speak. "I know I am mixed up. Should I talk? No, I will sit here and rub my fingers together, smoke another cigarette."

Oh yes, don't forget the illnesses, such as congestive heart failure. You're only forty-eight. There's a twenty percent chance of survival. "Well, doctor, guess you better do the surgery. Don't have anything to lose."

You wonder how he can keep going day after day after day, how he has the will to live with the horrendous hourly struggle just to survive in the world.

Seven years later, he's in a mental breakdown in the same hospital as Mom. Her baby, her little wounded bird, is here again for another open-heart surgery. How can he handle it? He's in the critical coronary unit, running through the hall naked, until he is subdued by the male nurses. How horribly terrified was he? What demons made him run while in critical condition, near death? But he has that damn will to live. He makes it through the massive open-heart surgery again. He defies all odds. He is known as the Miracle Man on the third floor. But be careful. He is mentally ill.

Loss. My mother lost her son to mental illness. She lost her flame for life. We wake to find what the day will bring; joy, terror, happiness, accomplishment, a successful family holiday or birthday. Would Mom actually get to enjoy all of us and our mentally ill family member?

I sat on the porch swing tonight reading my journal of 1994 when we moved to Oregon. I was finally with my family again after twenty-three years of living apart because of my career. I read from the first year we arrived, how happy I was to be here. Then the next page: He is in jail. He's back in hospital. He's on the street. His meds seem to be working great.

He spent the weekend with us. We laughed, went rafting down the river, hunted mushrooms, and went to a movie, all to be lost in the next two months, again, still, over and over and over.

Loss of sanity. Loss of showering. Loss of him. But through it all I can hate him sometimes, because of his self-medicating with drugs that are only adding to the trauma. But that hate lasts only until I stop, breathe, and know, he is the one that has the loss, a loss so great we can never imagine.

Our Mom passed away. He lost his angel. She was his momma. He is our baby brother. Mom and Dad fought all their married life to save their little boy from the demons that creep into his mind that he cannot control. He continues to fight not to lose his way every minute.

I speak of this loss for all the people who are afflicted with a brain disorder, people who have lost their dreams, their daily life, a movie, a football game, a memory of the daughter they had, a brunette young girl who said she would love him through it, only to realize that sometimes, not even the best of care, medicines, hospitals, or all of a family's love can accomplish such a task. We continue every day looking for the big puffy pink cloud in the sky that says "Found." You can know this loss only if you have a brain disorder or a loved one or friend who is afflicted with a brain disorder. Pray for their peace of mind.

2

Words

by John Hope

Current age: 38
Age at time of loss: 8

When I was eight years old, I watched my friend James die. Actually he wasn't my friend. In fact, I wanted him to die. His death was not what changed my life, though. My grandfather's words following James's death did that.

James's chipped front tooth, wild dark hair, and potty mouth were sandpaper to my church-boy life. Openly defiant toward everyone, he was the first kid I knew who cussed at a teacher. When we played flag football in P. E., he straight-armed short kids like me, laughed, and volleyed wads of mucus our way. Even when we were on the same team, he kicked our shins, and we hit the dirt. On his more lively days, he sat on our heads afterwards. To this day I taste the raw bitter flavor of Florida dirt on the back of my tongue when I think of his brutality.

I hated James.

But I didn't wish him death until he ripped off Friedrich's pants before school. The act was as random as his other attacks.

I sat outside my classroom before school with a copy of *In Search of a Shark* in my hand, my current favorite book. Friedrich raced up to me and chattered on and on in his thick German accent. His dad had just finished building him a go-cart, and he'd spent the previous evening doing doughnuts in an abandoned Kash n' Karry parking lot near his house. He had an unusually deep voice for an eight-year-old, and his excitement caused his voice to crack, which, combined with his choppy German syllables, made him impossible to fully understand, but his enthusiasm made up for it.

In the middle of Friedrich's tale, James emerged out of nowhere and yanked Friedrich's shorts and underwear down to his ankles.

Shocked, Friedrich stood frozen, stunned by his sudden nakedness.

James seized the chance and rammed his hand into Friedrich's back.

Friedrich's face smacked the pavement.

An entourage of giggling kids, boys and girls, laughed at the horrific performance, James leading the chorus.

Friedrich rolled to his back, grabbed his bloody face, and screamed, his shorts still wrapped around his ankles.

James topped his achievement by dropping a loogie on top of Friedrich's dirtied privates.

The crowd roared.

I pulled my legs in, squeezed them against my chest, and wished for James's death. I didn't care how, I just wanted him dead. Tears welled up, and my nose clogged. I held up my book and pretended to read, hoping no one, including James, noticed me. The words on the pages sparkled and meshed together. I silently cursed James's name.

My prayers were answered weeks later.

I rode in the passenger seat of my mom's giant brown Dodge Aspen. My mom, outfitted in her white and green crossing guard uniform, drove her normal route to my school down a traffic-jammed 54th Avenue. When we stopped along the two-lane road, I gazed out the window and spotted James and who I presumed was his mom pushing a stroller.

Their backs to me, they walked down the sidewalk to my school. James tossed a playground ball and caught it again as he hopped back and forth.

I thought of Friedrich and the scabbed face he'd lived with for the past few weeks. Hatred stewed inside me. I narrowed my eyes at James, imagining I could fire lasers out of my skull and fry unsuspecting jerks of my choosing.

James seemed oblivious to me, as he often did. He happily trotted along the sidewalk, advancing to the school faster than my mother and me in the car.

A minute later, traffic opened up ahead and we pulled forward.

Screech-thump.

The car ahead of us stopped.

Mom slammed on her brakes.

I looked to the side. No James.

Only eight years old, but I figured out the equation immediately. James had been hit, but neither the screeching tires nor the low thud were as bad as the sound that followed. James's mother let go a wail that tightened my spine and made my arms go numb. She abandoned the baby in the stroller and dashed out into the road.

Blocked by the car ahead of us, I couldn't see what she was doing. I only heard her screams.

A man stepped out of the car ahead. Another jumped out the passenger side and dashed toward the nearby apartments, I guessed to phone 911.

Minutes passed. Chaos reigned as people poured out of their cars. My stomach bubbled the morning's Life cereal.

Mom repeated, "Oh, my. Oh, my." She scared me the way she moved in nervous switches, grabbing the wheel, then her hair, then the seat, and then her mouth.

I grabbed the door handle.

"No," she snapped.

I released. I required no further explanation from her.

I sat, waiting. The tension nearly killed me.

A woman walked James's mother back to the sidewalk. She flailed her arms, babbled hysterically, and swung her body like she'd lost her mind.

A few cars moved next to us.

Mom tugged the wheel and checked her blind spot.

I asked, "We leaving?"

"We're not involved."

Our car circled around the car that had hit James. We inched forward. As we approached the front of the car, I peered out the window.

There he was, James, lying on his back, his legs and arms crisscrossing his body in strange, inhuman angles. The ball he had been playing with lay near his feet and rocked back and forth, disturbed by an invisible wind. His body was parallel to us and his head faced us.

In a brief instant, I saw it. James opened his eyes. In that second, no one in the entire world could have seen it except for me. The people loitering outside stood on the opposite side of James, staring at the back of James's head, and in that moment, I swear, James stared straight at me, not at the road, not at our car, and not at the door. Me.

A second later, we pulled forward. I blinked, and James's eyes were closed.

When I got to school, I floated on a cloud. I remained in that state for the next hour or so. Class started. The pledge. The morning announcements. Spelling quiz. Teacher at the chalkboard. I floated and felt nothing.

Our elderly guidance counselor, Mrs. Schultz, stepped in and whispered something to our teacher. The old woman broke the horrible news to my class. James had been seriously hurt and was never coming back to school. "No, Mary," her scratchy, smoker's voice explained. "He's not at the doctor's. He's not getting a cast."

Girls cried. Boys stared.

James had died.

That evening I sat at the table staring at one of my dad's hand-patted enormous hamburgers surrounded by half-burnt French fries. My grandparents had joined us for dinner, which took much of the attention off me. Parts of their chatter worked their way into my brain.

Kids don't listen to adults these days.

They dash into the street without thinking.

The lack of parental supervision these days is disgraceful.

Teenage moms are horrible.

Nobody takes responsibility.

I stood from the table.

Dad said, "You haven't touched your burger."

"Um…" was all I could get out. I shook my head and raced to my bedroom.

My room sanctuary allowed honesty to hit. I cried, a deep bellowing cry. I couldn't breathe in enough air. My chest pressed in on me. My body shivered.

The door squeaked.

My back to the door, I wiped my face, trying to hide the tears that I knew the intruder must have heard.

When I spun, the face surprised me. Of all people that would've chased me into my room, I never expected Pap, my grandfather.

I stood. I held my breath.

Pap was an enormous man. With white hair and sagging muscles, he was a giant even to adults. In his youth he could lift two men dangling from an iron rod. People feared him, and his gentle, barking voice made them listen.

He stepped forward.

I stepped back.

He waited, staring with deep patience.

I knew he wanted me to speak.

I tried, but my lips felt glued together and my jaws rattled. Still, I worked at it, breathed, and forced the words out. "I…I wanted him to die."

He nodded and stepped forward.

The need to retreat pulled at me, but I couldn't move. My hands tightened into fists. A tidal wave of crying was on the verge of cresting. My body shuddered at its coming.

Pap stopped inches from me. He didn't ask details. He didn't want James's name or how I knew him or why I wanted him dead. He didn't tell me to talk about it.

Instead, Pap placed a hand on my shoulder and said the most unexpected words I could have imagined. "Sometimes it's hard."

Those words were the heaviest I'd ever heard in my life. They crushed me.

Tears flooded out. I fell into Pap's massiveness.

He pressed me against him.

We stood there for a long time, my small body melting into Pap's. I shook as I listened to the thump of his heartbeat against my face.

Decades have passed, yet I carry the memory with me day after day and cling onto those three words Pap had gifted me with that evening. That massive phrase has been a torch for me throughout my darkness. The day I was alone along the side of the highway in the middle of a 200-mile road race. The many months I worried myself into an ulcer when I was jobless, buried under a mortgage, expecting my firstborn, yet trying to convince my wife everything was going to be okay. And the day I said good-bye to Pap, his ashes interred in the marbled blue vase on the mantel.

Every day I think about the power of Pap's words. Many times I'm floored by what words can do to both the reader and the writer. I've often attempted to sculpt my own phrases that I hoped would tap a trickle of truth in someone else's life, but without a doubt, the most powerful words that have ever crossed my mind were a simple phrase a grandfather spoke into the heart of a small eight-year-old in the quiet of his bedroom.

"Sometimes it's hard."

* * *

John Hope is an award-winning short story, children's book, middle grade, young adult, and nonfiction writer. His work appears in paperback, hardback, audiobook, and multiple short story collections.

All of his published works, including over 30 short stories and 11 books, can be found at www.johnhope-writing.com. This website also includes free downloads of his presentations and teaching material to assist educators in using his books in the classroom.

3

From Broken Heart to Open Heart

by Emily Keese

Current age: 52
Age at time of loss: 33

*Certain names have been shortened to initials for confidentiality purposes.

G rowing up in a loving, Christian home in a small Texas town, I had dreams of traveling the world, marrying a good man, raising a family, and living happily ever after, all in that order. I never realized then how life could be ever changing.

Fast forward through my happy childhood, rebellious teenage years, a failed marriage (one beautiful son, Slade, was born), graduation with a pharmacy degree, and loss of my mother.

I was thirty-three years old when I woke up on December 4, 1996, and started my typical morning. I woke my only son up so he could get ready for school, kissed my new husband Wayne (married for six months), and we discussed our plans to visit his teenage son, *D. K., who was in a Canton drug rehab at the time. Wayne planned to get home early, get Slade ready, and as soon as I got off of work we would leave for Canton.

Wayne left for work. Slade and I were talking about Christmas and the gifts he wanted. He asked me if he could ride his new bike that was locked in another room (apparently he had peeked). I told him we hadn't bought him one, and he giggled, kissed me good-bye, and walked the block to school. I went on to work.

As soon as work was over I drove the few minutes home looking forward to our little road trip. As I rounded the corner by our house, I saw yellow police tape and police cruisers in our driveway. My heart raced as I got out of the car not knowing what was happening. About that time I saw Wayne coming out to meet me. At that moment my life was shattered.

Wayne told me that Slade, only eleven years old, was shot and killed during a robbery of our house. Slade walked the block home from school around 3:00. When Wayne arrived home early and walked into our bedroom, he saw that Slade was tied up with an air hose and had been shot. Wayne called 911, but Slade was already gone.

I walked into our house. It was in shambles, partly from the person ransacking the house looking for things, but also from the blood on the carpet area and fingerprint dust everywhere. The police questioned me about Slade and asked if we suspected anyone. They finally left.

Wayne's parents arrived, and I called my sister and father, and we went to Wayne's parents' house. I knew my life would never be the same, but I had no idea what I was really in for.

That day I turned my back on God and my faith. I could not understand why He would let such a thing happen to anyone. The next few weeks were very hard. Lots of tears, anger, and fear. We had to plan a funeral for Slade and attend it. My only memory of that day is kissing Slade on the forehead. Our friends returned all the Christmas gifts we had purchased for Slade.

We bought a travel trailer and parked it in front of Wayne's parents' house, because we could never stay in our home again. We had to pack up our belongings and clean out Slade's room. It's amazing the things an eleven-year-old hides in his room; fireworks, matches, a letter written to a company saying he had ordered a helicopter but he hadn't received it, more than a hundred dollars in a sock, and other personal items. I think I cried the entire day. Our family and friends went home after a few weeks, and life had to continue.

We went back to work and tried to find some normalcy. I was not normal at all. I was a wreck. I cried if I heard a baby cry. I cried if I saw a child. I envisioned my son crying for help. I was scared to stay alone. I couldn't talk to Wayne about Slade, because Wayne saw Slade that day, and I knew it hurt Wayne to talk about him. I couldn't talk to anyone, because everyone would cry, and I couldn't stand making them upset. I was angry and felt very guilty I was not there to take care of my son. A few months went by, and I finally broke down. I took a six-week leave from work and attended some counseling. I thought, *"Now I'm cured."* *Not.* I was still angry and my compassion was gone, not good for a pharmacist. I tried to forget it all.

A day later, on December 5, 1996, *R. A. called his father and told him he killed Slade. His father picked him up and took him to the police station. R. A. confessed to the murder and was placed in jail awaiting trial.

R. A. was a sixteen-year-old boy who lived across the street from our house and ran around with my stepson, Slade and R. A. knew each other. R. A. had been kicked out of school and his own home. He broke into our house because he needed money.

On May 1997 the murder trial began. Another nightmare: Wayne couldn't attend the trial with me, because he was considered a witness, since he found Slade. I have a few memories of the trial, most not pleasant. I learned that R. A. tied Slade up and left him alive, only to return to our house and shoot him. Autopsy photos showed that R. A. shot him five times. I had to listen to details of the whole incident. Finally the trial was over. R. A. was sentenced to eighty-five years and would have to serve thirty-eight years before he was eligible for parole. If released he will be deported to the country of his birth. Another child lost.

In 1998, my father passed away and my anger at God increased.

Another eight years passed, and I wasn't the same person I was just a few short years before. I was still very angry, and it consumed me. I tried to ruin my marriage and my life in general. On a family visit I had a conversation with my brother-in-law and told him I was tired of being angry. As a pastor, he told me that we needed to find a church family. The very next week a good friend Brian invited Wayne to an event at Stonewater Church. Wayne attended, and on the next Sunday we both attended church. I cried the entire service. I was hardheaded and ignored the huge sign.

The next week, the same thing happened. I finally gave up. God was calling me home. Within a few weeks, Wayne and I attended a marriage seminar. One evening I walked up a lane to a cross on a hill. The cross was shining in the moonlight. I broke down and prayed to God for forgiveness and to give me the grace needed to forgive R. A.

In 2008, Wayne and I took a mission trip down the Amazon River with our church. During that trip, my faith in God grew and my outlook on life took a turn. I realized on the trip that no matter what had happened in my life, there were a lot of people who were less fortunate than me.

I registered in 2009 to begin the mediation process, which can take years in Texas, because of the limited number of mediators. A year went by, and a guy from the state called and said he was visiting R. A. and he would get back with me in a few months.

My mediator contacted me in 2011 and told me that R. A. had refused to see me and we could only exchange letters. I was disappointed, because I needed to see him in person to ensure I had forgiven him completely.

My letter written on January 27, 2011:

R.,

I want to start this letter with brutal honesty. My life, along with my family's, was forever changed by the decision you made to kill Slade. I was devastated. Slade was my only child and my heart and soul. A piece of me was torn away and can never be replaced. I will never get to see my son graduate, fall in love, get married, or hold his children.

The pain and guilt I felt for not being there to protect my baby consumed me immediately. Over the years, the pain and guilt were replaced with anger and rage. For eight years, I dwelled on the reasons why God was punishing me, and my anger was ruining my life.

A few years ago, Wayne and I started going to church regularly, and my heart began to change. I have prayed and prayed about my anger and unwillingness to forgive. My thoughts and prayers have now changed from focusing on myself to focusing on others.

My heart breaks for you and your family. For you, one horrible decision took away your freedom and all you could've done and experienced as a young man. For your family, they also lost a son and all the experiences involved.

I wanted desperately to tell you all this in person, but the letter will have to do for now. R., I have forgiven you for taking Slade's life, and my hope is that you will forgive yourself and help other teens in your position. People are continually asking why I would forgive you, and my only response is that God gave me the gift of forgiveness, so in my heart it is only right to forgive you. By the grace of God, my life has been blessed.

During my journey to forgiveness, I did a lot of reading, and one book's exercise included writing a poem through your eyes. I will share it with you.

—Emily Keese

Through an Offender's Eyes

Fear and anger have stolen my life.
My choices as a young man have caused much strife.
The gun went off; I killed a child.
My thoughts and feelings are running wild.
Eighty-five years is what the jury said.
Horrible fears flooded my head.
Spending my life behind steel bars will,
I hope, heal part of my scars.
Forgive me, Father, for my terrible sin,
and let my heart be open for you to come in.
After many years inside this place,
I am finally accepting God's forgiving grace.

In response to my letter, almost a year later, I received this letter written on December 4, 2011, from R. A.:

Dear Emily,

I sit here and struggle to find just the right words to express exactly how I feel. I'm so, so grateful that you sacrificed your time to write and even contact me. I promise you that these simple words do not come close to showing you how truly grateful I really am for your presence. Once again, thank you so much!

I cannot imagine how you must have felt to lose your only child. I can only begin to understand how losing a child can devastate a mother's entire life.

My life experiences have given me a huge understanding of a sense of loss. From the smallest to the greatest things in life, such as being able to walk around barefoot in the grass or being able to go outside to appreciate the beauty of the stars in the dark sky. However, nothing that I've ever lived in my life and experienced will surpass your experiences with losing your child. I hate that life took such a horrible twist for you and your family. I wish none of us had to lose anything. I wish there was some sort of "prayer" or "magical words" that would replace your loss.

I also wanted to say all this so desperately to you in person; however I cannot. I pray that you can find it in your heart to understand. There are a lot of things that we both have a need to express. I truly believe that one day God will bring us together. I await that day to come.

I've read your letter over and over, and each time it brought me closer to understanding you, who you were, what you have been through, and furthermore who you have become. The beauty of your blessings you spoke in your letter is expressed within each of your words and thoughts. I must say your letter is by far the most important and the most meaningful letter I've received within the last fifteen years. I will keep your thoughts dearly close to my heart.

My empathy for you and your family is consciously living within me, each and every day of my existence. My family has also kept and keeps you and your family in their prayers.

I wanted to relay to you about some of my accomplishments while in prison. I've earned an associate's degree and am working on a bachelor's degree at the University of Houston-Clear Lake. I also plan to study for a master's in the near future.

You spoke of reaching out to teens. I have been, for a while now, putting together a nonprofit site for reaching out to troubled teenagers. It's just an idea for now, but I'm planning to have it up and running within the next two years. My goal is to help just one kid, and if blessed, to help many kids.

I'm sharing my accomplishments with you to show you how this experience has changed my life, as well as how I've learned to help others. I have many ideas and have much desire to fill my past, present, and future life with meaning and purpose.

I don't know exactly what your intentions are beyond this letter. I wonder what may come next, if anything at all. I hate to think that there is a sign at the end that reads Dead End; however, I pray that your step toward my life has blessed you with better understanding and meaning as it has done for me in my life. I pray that I never lose whatever part of you that decided to reach out for me. I hope that I have given you a clear idea of how much your presence has affected my life. Thank you again for all your words and thoughts. I continue to keep you and your family in my thoughts and prayers. Until another time, I pray that God continues to bless you with guidance and understanding.

Please take care.

—R. A.

I was still disappointed in not getting a face-to-face meeting, but I had to continue with life and find closure.

Wayne and I continued to receive God's blessings throughout the years. Wayne's company was very profitable; our jobs were great; our health was good; and our marriage was strong.

I began going to Kenya in 2010, to participate in medical missions, and I loved every minute of each trip. I have been blessed by all the children in Eldoret, and my heart is full.

Wayne and I had a dream to own a catamaran and retire on the ocean. We ordered a boat in 2012, and after many prayers, decided to use our boat to reach and help others. We named her *Manna*, which means gift from heaven.

In 2013, Wayne traveled to South Africa to sail *Manna* back to the USA for the Miami Boat Show 2014. While Wayne was in South Africa, the mediator reached out to me and said R. A. wanted to see me. I was elated. Finally after so many years, God had answered my prayers. Texas Mediation requires several sessions to allow victims and offenders to meet. The process took a few months, and then our date was set for July 24, 2014.

Wayne and I met with the mediator in Houston, Texas, the morning of the July 24. We drove to the prison where R. A. was, and in an attempt to calm me down, we took a tour of the prison first, and then Wayne stayed in the warden's office.

The only fear I had in the entire process was the minute I walked away from Wayne and had to face R. A. on my own, but I was ready. I carried only a piece of paper with a list of points to discuss with him. The backside of the paper had this verse on it: "May the grace of the Lord Jesus Christ, and the love of God, and the fellowship of the Holy Spirit be with you." 2 Corinthians 13:14.

I walked with the mediators into a room with only a table with four chairs. We all sat down on one side of the table, and the waiting began. Only a few minutes later, a guard arrived and said R. A. was coming in.

I stood up and faced the door.

As the door opened, I saw a scared sixteen-year-old (even though he was thirty-four by then) come in with his head down. He looked up at me. I smiled, and he never put his head down again. We sat down, and he asked if he could read me a letter first. His letter was as follows:

Regardless of how many times I sit here, intending to think of the right words to express precisely how I feel, I fail with each attempt. There isn't a word in the English language or any other language, for that matter, that could be translated into expressing the degree of remorse I live with about the circumstances of our visit. Thank you for enduring the long journey for this meeting. I have prayed for many nights for this moment, and I am extremely grateful that you have blessed me with this opportunity to be at your mercy. I understand that it takes great strength, fortitude, and valor to place yourself face to face with the individual who robbed your son of the opportunity to live and choose the course he could have charted for his future.

On Dec 4, 1996, my selfish action caused you and your family to suffer a tremendous loss. I cannot imagine the heartbreak, depression, loneliness, emptiness, anger, and pain I induced in everyone.

Countless times I've thought about the only-if statement. I wish there were some miraculous powers that could place him back in the comfort of your arms. Nothing or no one could ever replace the precious gift that I've caused you to lose. Although I've never been a parent, I comprehend with complete sincerity that my actions shattered your future as a mother, for a mother's love for her child is incomparable to any other love in existence.

As I've said, there aren't the words to express how incredibly sorry I am for all the pain and suffering I've caused you and your family. I don't think any length of time I spend in prison can ever be enough to justify the loss of your son. I pray that one day or at some point of your life you can grant me forgiveness for my thoughtless, ignorant, and senseless actions.

I could see the remorse in R. A.'s face as he read this letter to me and asked me for my forgiveness. I told him that I had forgiven him a long time before, and it was time he forgave himself.

We talked about that fateful day that happened many years before, about my family now, and his aging parents. We talked about what he was doing in prison to help others and continue his education. When our time was close to being over, he asked me to tell him about Slade, what his hopes and dreams had been.

Neither of us wanted the visit to end. As I left, all I wanted to do was to hug him and tell him he would be okay, but it was not allowed. I left the prison with a heart full of grace and empathy.

When I returned to *Manna*, there was one last thing I needed to do before I closed that chapter in my life. I sent the following letter to R. A.'s parents:

This letter has been on my mind since my visit with your son. I want to start by saying that I am sorry that all of us are in this horrible situation. I know that what happened was no fault of yours.

Our lives have been changed tremendously over the last eighteen years. My heart has a huge part missing from my loss, and I know you two have felt the same loss over the years. Neither of us gets to experience those special times with our boys that we should have.

I just want you both to know that I forgave R. many years ago, thanks to God's mercy and grace. I was scared that anger would overwhelm me when I saw your son, but when he walked in, all I felt was compassion. Yes, he took away Slade's life, but in turn he took his own life.

He read me his letter with remorse and emotion. I am proud of what R. has accomplished while incarcerated. It took an extreme amount of courage and strength for him to be with me, and during our visit I came to realize that R. is a good man who made a huge mistake as a child. He did tell me how much he loved you and how supportive you have been through the years.

Even though R. is in the system, I believe he will continue to do good works. His remaining sentence is in God's hands, and I will continue to pray for R. daily.

It took six months before I received this letter from R.'s parents:

> We are both so sorry for all the pain our family has caused your family. All our lives have changed and will never be the same. Thank you for making your peace with our son. I am sure he feels the same.
>
> Time will heal, but what happened will never be forgotten. Slade will always be in our hearts forever. May Allah rest his soul in peace.
>
> It took a lot of strength and courage for both of you to visit. I will leave all in Allah's hands and continue to pray for Slade and his family.
>
> Thank you once again for your forgiveness toward our son.
>
> May Allah bless you.

This long chapter of my life can finally say "The End." I lost my son, but I have watched my nieces graduate, get married, and start families of their own. I have watched my stepson, D. K., grow into a God-loving man and a good father. I married a wonderful man. I have and am still traveling the world aboard *Manna*.

My heart will always have a special place for Slade, but God has given me the grace and strength to open my heart up for others who are in need. We use *Manna* for chartering for humanitarian needs, such as delivering supplies to other islands and free missionary vacations through our nonprofit organization, Manna for Missionaries.

I have learned one very important thing: don't ever let life's circumstances overtake you; rely on your faith in God. "I can do all things through Christ who strengthens me." Philippians 4:13.

My childhood dreams that were lost many years ago have now all been fulfilled, maybe not exactly as I thought, but nevertheless achieved. I am truly blessed and living happily ever after.

4

A More Rugged Soul

by James Robert Starkey

Current age: 42
Age at time of loss: 17

There remains a mystical sorrow that permeates one's soul after taking a life. Fermented by the combination of time and anguish, such a feeling brews into more of a poison than an intoxicant that continually infects every facet of a murderer's life. I am indeed still a person— monster I may be to some - as I seek not to shamelessly sling stock nouns and slack verbs to those willing to communicate with me, but to relay to those who are moments away from making those very mistakes that resulted in the unspoken promise of other options evaporating.

I could repeat "I am sorry" until the power of speech leaves me, but will it ever be enough? Better men than me will judge the sincerity of my pleas, similar to the men who decided that I, at the age of seventeen, no longer deserved my freedom. Do I deserve to be in prison? Absolutely! I committed a crime and a debt must be paid; however, this man of forty-two years of age now wonders at what point does justice turn into vengeance?

Questions may linger like the haunts of yesterday's mistakes, mine far more tragic and horrific than most, melancholy-infused moments fossilized by unreachable answers to what most folks long to know: How valuable is freedom? I believe I know the answer all too well. I have failed, and I have done so in spectacular fashion. I am the sole architect of my failures.

It is no coincidence that these decades of being incarcerated are filled with disappointment in myself for what I have done as well as what I have failed to do. Through the act of callousness, intentional or not, I have robbed the local community of the promise held in a young life.

True, I may have lost my freedom, but in the process, a family lost something far more valuable.

With every loss in our lives a void is created. Whether enormous in size or elaborate in its shape, it exists. Some people accommodate this intruder by constructing a wall between it and their everyday lives. The hallucination does not serve anyone well. As hypnotic as known comforts may be, a lesson I learned is this: ignoring such a void does nothing more than allow such emptiness to increase exponentially, consuming everything in its path. A void soon turns into a vacuum. Nature, abhorring a vacuum, fills it with substance from the squalid portions of our minds. The two most common emotions to fill that void are equal measures of fear and regret.

There are 2.1 million Americans housed in correctional facilities, which illuminates the fact those of us identified by an inmate number have failed our fellow citizens. In a manner extravagant or mundane, shameless or remorseful, our actions have produced a just result. While I consider it a minor miracle that I continue to draw breath, others curse each exhale.

Prison is an environment purposefully designed to be both restrictive and oppressive. The wretchedness of our conditions can break the strongest person. No matter how well prepared, no matter how well armored, every human being has a breaking point. Polished attributes I once cherished are exposed as faults. Undeterred by unsolicited advice, I embrace what fear has shown to me.

The reflection I see shocks me.

Consumed by anger, blinded by a convoluted sense of justice I believed, as a teenager no less, I had all the answers. I ignored the whispered guidance that once had enveloped me and thrust my soul into a situation I was ill equipped to combat. Flailing about, engaging in the most brutal of acts, I removed a soul from the face of the earth. The finality of my actions was disregarded at that moment. An irresistible opportunity, glittering like fool's gold, presented itself, and I failed to make a wise choice.

Through this experience I have learned that our lives are governed by the choices we make. Years later I find myself probing for the prospect of redemption, yet fear attempts to grip me again. Its steely-clawed fingers simply pass through my flesh, making no contact, finding no purchase. Why? It is indeed a terrible thing to live in fear, but it is far more dreadful to live without it. The absence of the caution it inherently provides, the injection of suspicion into the mindset of even the most happy-go-lucky of folks, no longer tempers the impulsive decisions made.

Prolonged incarceration distills fear from us as if it were some ruinous substance to be rejected with no consideration of its value. It's not as if imprisoned souls could be humiliated any further.

Those who remain wicked prey on those who remain optimistic for a better life, regardless of where they lay their heads at night. Predators within a cage fear no retribution, and those viewed as targets cope as best they can. Fear, once entrenched, becomes difficult to evict. Some wield its influence to force others to do what they would otherwise not do. Some watch as others crumble underneath threats looming before them. What is inevitable is that fear will have inhabited some portion of a prisoner's life and then, its tenuous grasp on what one holds dear is released, flickers for but a moment, a solemn curse uttered, it is gone. At that point in a person's incarceration, the void is at once absent of fear. A seemingly marvelous turn of events until, upon closer inspection, fear may have vacated the vacuum. However, it absconded with something far more valuable, hope.

In some sense, what I did may be considered the perfect crime. No witnesses. No evidence. Law enforcement officers had no clue what happened. I would not be writing this from a prison cell had I not turned myself in, provided a complete confession, and pled guilty. When asked if I feel remorse, I generally refer to the previous sentence. Regret is perhaps the most difficult portion of my journey. I feel regret not because that is what someone told me to say or because I think that is what you want to hear, but because I truly regret my actions.

I do regret what I have done and the subsequent pain that must have dominated every aspect of my victim's family's lives. While you may not be able to see the look on my face, please believe there is sincerity in this ink.

Regret, unlike fear, does not often entrench itself ever so firmly into our lives. Instead it returns at irregular intervals to haunt us. It separates us from a more productive and happier life.

As intriguing a life incarcerated may be to some people, what astounds me, without fail, is how startled the average person becomes to learn how truly horrific the loss of freedom may be. Some media outlets have referred to prolonged incarceration as "the other death penalty." Such a description is eerily accurate, since some cease to live and instead simply exist in the rawest and simplest manner imaginable. Warehousing and indifference replaced any wistful notions of rehabilitation made long ago.

Almost all progress, from educating yourself to maintaining your humanity in an inhumane environment, must be initiated and completed by yourself. Very little assistance is offered by the Department of Corrections. We prisoners may have lost our freedom, but the powers that be have lost interest in the funding necessary to run a prison properly. We are forgotten, unpolished outcasts by those who do not regret the decision to spend $2.10 a day to feed one imprisoned soul. I do not regret the fact that I may never taste a steak again, but the fact I took away another human being's ability to do so.

Much of what I regretted missing immediately following my arrest is the product of a teenager's mind. Missing prom, no longer being a member of the debate team, not spending time with my friends are obviously superficial concerns when compared to my incomprehensible actions.

At the time, in my cluttered brain, the condensation of teenage angst combined with a poorly nourished sense of self-esteem resulted in the grossly underestimated seriousness of the situation. How could I recognize the enormity of the circumstances when what sensibilities I possessed were addled by my inability to comprehend the consequences of unchecked impulse control issues? Freedom was far from my mind. It was far from my mind when I pulled the trigger. It was far from my mind when I contemplated taking my own life with that very firearm. It was far from my mind even when I was first handcuffed. I never gave freedom much consideration, until it was gone.

As a boy of seventeen I felt I was indestructible. I felt I was already in possession of a more rugged soul. How wrong I was!

When I stood before a court and recounted the events leading to my decision to dispense justice that, in my feeble reckoning, did not resemble revenge, many who listened were intrigued. When someone abducted and raped my girlfriend, she was not relieved only of her freedom. She lost more than that. Much more. She was robbed of her innocence. She was denied a peaceful night of sleep for decades. She lost all interest in her education; a once bright girl could no longer string together a coherent sentence. She refused to socialize with anyone other than me. I tremulously forced myself to remain calm and in control. The calmness I could fake. The in-control portion of the façade soon surrendered to my lost fantasy of happily ever after.

Some hard truths were learned that night. Blind anger, distilled into frustration, did not produce a tasty elixir but instead became bitter as quinine. I envisioned some elegant variation of sacrificing myself in the moment for her future well-being. Instead I made myself the most innovatively stupid teenager on the planet. Once simply an awkward boy, I was presented with the loathsome reality of a life without freedom, without privacy, and with daily exposure to unspeakable brutality.

The sickening enormity of how many folks were negatively affected by my simple action produced an amnesia of sorts in me. My highly selective memory futilely attempted to rationalize an irrational event. As a judge calculated exactly what cost I would pay, I was acutely aware of what I had done, not the romanticized version, but the truth that led me to detest myself. I heard the anguished moan of the family that would forever mourn. I knew I'd upset a tranquil community and exposed it to homicide. My future would forever be haunted by my mistakes. The secret shame I felt was not so secret anymore. The masses questioned the who, what, and why of such a horrific event. Folks hoped for some utterance from me. All were disappointed as my prolonged silence was not a form of self-preservation, but because my voice was suspended by something far more disconcerting; unresolved regret.

Rarely will an extended stint in prison transition a person into a better person. This menagerie of volatile creatures consumes rational thought and compassion and exhales insanity and repulsiveness. Most prisoners refuse to stop, if only for the briefest of moments, to conduct an objective evaluation of their strengths and flaws. Instead they change for the worse and allow their anger to reach critical mass, devastating all in their wake.

I managed to avoid inhabiting the worse portions of my character, and now, after a quarter century of incarceration, I have succeeded only in becoming much more cynical than I once was, and I laugh far less often than I once did. Though my current self is not the skeletal apparition I feared it would become, those changes I have detected are certainly sobering. I no longer have a fixation on perfecting my future, for I am acutely aware I am a fortunate man indeed even to have a future. When friends ask me if I am saddened by the possibility I may never have children, I gently remind them my victim will never have the opportunity to have children. There will be no future incarnations of such a gentle soul.

The world that once existed prior to my arrest, everything from technology to fashion to etiquette either no longer exists or has changed drastically, as have I. My admittedly lofty dream of becoming a cardiothoracic surgeon evaporated as quickly as the life I took. More than dreams were lost that night. Two lives, once laden with hope and promise, exist no more.

One man lies in a grave and the other lies in his bed at night haunted by the actions of a lesser self. It may be true that I remain among the living; however, my life is composed solely of nightmares. These nightmares I have experienced since I decided to take a life, pales, though, in comparison to the anguish and suffering my victim's family continues to live with to this day.

Many changes occur in a man's life from the age of seventeen to the age of forty-two. With every gray hair I mourn the passing of a young man whose hair will never change color.

Somehow I have managed to cope with the reality that is this concrete and steel cocoon in which I find myself. I have learned hard truths about how delicate life is, as well as how fragile the human soul may become after decades of neglect and indifference. I wish I had received the advice that encouraged me to examine why I was feeling the way I was feeling and address flaws before time and frustration rendered them fatal. Futures were altered. Some dreams were shattered and lost, and other dreams were abandoned.

It is my sincerest wish that his family has found peace and closure and that I may develop a more rugged soul.

5

Escape from the Abyss: One Woman's Journey Beyond Grief

by Diane Payne

Current age: 62
Age at time of loss: 50

A bottomless abyss stretched from my feet almost to the horizon, like a sinister lake with a rocky shoreline, except that "shoreline" didn't represent the limits of my vision, but the limits of my reality. One day I opened my eyes, and that abyss was all that was left of my life.

To make matters worse, I had to dodge occasional sniper fire. I never knew where it was going to come from next, how long it would last, or why it was aimed at me. Regardless, I had to stay awake, stay alert to danger, and keep moving, albeit with no other purpose driving me than the primal instinct to survive.

I was exhausted, yet too terrified to let down my guard. I was cut off from everything I once knew, with no hope of regaining normalcy. My world had shrunk down to a nightmarish scenario where nothing was safe and there was no future to contemplate. That future had disappeared in the blink of an eye, along with my old life.

That was my experience with early widowhood, all of the first and second years. It's important to stress this point, because those who have never lost a spouse often have the misguided impression that "normal" grieving lasts maybe six months before you shake it off, pick up the pieces, and move on. Banish that notion. It's different for everyone. There is no set timeline, and grieving is very much one step forward, two steps back. It takes as long as it takes, and it hurts like hell for a long, long time.

I'm sixty-two, and I have been a widow for eleven years. Though I'm no longer actively grieving my loss, I still love, miss, and talk about my husband regularly. I always will.

The horizons of my life have long since expanded far beyond the horrible scenario I described, but they did so only because I forced myself to reach out for help, taking an active role in grief recovery. After the first lonely, fear-filled year of skirting the abyss, I sought therapy, joined a few grief support groups, and took part in a couple of intensive workshops. I discovered a supportive online community of widows and widowers who seemed just as lost, damaged, and desperate as I felt. I formed new friendships with other people struggling with loss and the need to rebuild and restore order to their lives. I did a ton of self-exploration and had many new experiences while trying to figure out who I was, now that I was no longer one half of a couple.

Doug and I had been happily married for twenty-five years when he died at age fifty-five. The type II diabetes he had not taken seriously enough since his diagnosis at about age forty, caught up to him in a big way when he came down with a nasty virus one winter day. Weakened by disease, decades of smoking, and being out of shape, Doug's major organs rapidly began shutting down in response to the virus's assault. He spent more than a month in an ICU before exceeding the limits of medical intervention. I was fifty years old and alone at 5 a.m. on the thirty-ninth day of the ordeal when I found myself making the shocking, horrific decision to disconnect my soul mate and best friend from life support.

We had just embarked on what was to have been an exciting new chapter in our lives. For two decades, we had lived in the sprawling city of Atlanta, Georgia, where our demanding careers firmly anchored us. For much of that time, though, we had dreamed of owning a log cabin in the Blue Ridge Mountains that we could escape to for relaxing, indulgent weekends. The peace and quiet of the mountains and the slower, easygoing pace of life called sweetly to us. Even though land was cheap, we were still renting an apartment in the city and couldn't afford a second home. Finally in 2004, the time was right, and we purchased a modest little cabin. Oh, the plans we made for that place, the hours spent scheming and dreaming about all the ways it would make our lives much more enjoyable! We had spent only three weekends happily making our cabin into a cozy hideaway, when Doug fell seriously ill. All those plans suddenly derailed.

When my world crashed and burned with Doug's death nearly six weeks later, I realized I had no idea how to be just me. After spending half my life married, I had little left of me as an individual. I no longer recognized myself, and it was frightening. When had I so disappeared into being half of a couple that I had ceased to exist as an independent person capable of handling her own life? I had always been somewhat contemptuous of people who didn't seem to have a mind of their own and simply followed others blindly. Now it seemed to me that I had been fooling myself. I was one of them. Without Doug, I didn't know what to do with myself, what kind of persona to have. I was an empty shell, a blank slate, and the future was a soupy gray fog.

My loss of self was particularly disturbing, because I had been raised by a feminist, working mother who actively fought for women's rights. Total dependency on a man was definitely not cool. My parents had a fairly unorthodox marriage in which my mother was the chief breadwinner, rationing money out to my father. While I wasn't militant about feminism, I prided myself on being more independent than many of my peers. Doug and I spent a fair amount of time apart during our marriage. Not only did our jobs see to that, but each of us had our own interests, and we pursued them enthusiastically. It therefore made me uncomfortable to think that without my man, I had nothing, no real purpose in life, and no worthwhile future. I felt like I had betrayed feminism.

How could there possibly be a future without Doug beside me? Why should I care what happened to me now? Surely I would just dry up and blow away.

But I was still here, though I didn't want to be. I wished that I would die in my sleep. I decided after some thought that I would not kill myself, because my family was already devastated enough by Doug's death. I couldn't deliberately add to their anguish, but oh God, how I hoped that someone would take matters into their own hands and kill me in a traffic accident or murder me. There I was, just ripe for the picking, begging, in fact, to be targeted, but no one obliged. Shit!

Everything was a struggle during my abyss-centric time. I had never handled the household finances. While Doug was still fighting for his life in the hospital, I paid the bills that arrived in the mail, and then, realizing that our situation was going to be a long-term one, I began sorting through all of our files to familiarize myself with what we owed, to whom, and when payments were due.

This activity became more frenzied as winter turned to spring outside the hospital walls and tax season loomed. When Doug died on March 16, I spent a week or so huddled with my family and friends celebrating his life, feeling stunned, but glad that he had meant so much to so many people. I then channeled my anxiety into finding all the documents needed to compute our taxes. I had not handled taxes since I was single. I knew that Doug had invested the money we'd both saved over the years, setting up IRAs, a 401k, etc., and I worried about tracking them all down before April 15. I was embarrassed by how little I, as a fifty-year-old woman, knew about what was required for tax preparation, but with my father-in-law's help, I scraped together the bare necessities and prayed that H&R Block could make sense of the documents without asking too many questions I couldn't answer. Somehow the taxes got filed, even though I forgot to include a check for tax due when I mailed my return to the IRS.

As I continued to pay bills and fill out the endless forms required to apply for Doug's pension, establish myself as the administrator of his estate, and collect the money in various life insurance policies, I was alarmed to notice that the balance in our checking account had dwindled to nearly nothing. Doug's paychecks had stopped shoring it up, and mine alone couldn't cover everything, especially given the recent purchase of the cabin. Duh! It makes perfect sense that this would happen, and a normal person would have seen the problem coming, but a new widow's brain is far from normal. Apart from staving off the IRS and various creditors by throwing money and paperwork their way as required, I wasn't looking forward or strategizing at all. Doug's last paycheck served as a harsh reality check for me. He was really gone. He wasn't coming home. Ever. No matter how well I handled everything by myself, my little fantasy under which I'd been operating dissolved.

I secured a financial advisor and was relieved to find out that Doug had done a good job in growing our money over the years. The checking account was replenished and my fears calmed about having to sell the cabin that represented our dreams.

Bills, taxes, and estate matters aside, I was also terribly ill equipped to deal with the firestorm of grief and loneliness that was assaulting me.

I had grown up in an Irish Catholic family that didn't deal well with feelings. Emotions were considered embarrassing and frowned upon in our household. We kept them to ourselves as much as possible. Anger came out in dramatic bursts here and there and was very scary, even when I was the one who was angry, because there was no discernable lead-up to the outburst. It seemed to come out of nowhere. Words were the weapons, not fists, and they were used as deftly as knives. But tears? Hugs? Heartfelt discussions of how we felt about each other and what we needed? No. Not encouraged.

Fortunately Doug and his family were much more touchy-feely, and thanks to them, I had enjoyed decades of hugs, handholding, and even a few emotional talks as a married woman. I was still emotionally stunted though. I had great difficulty allowing myself to cry or show anyone else the depths of my despair. I put on "a good face" and insisted that I was okay. I might talk some about the loneliness and all the surreal aspects of outliving my life partner, but I saved the brokenhearted sobbing, the panicked gasps for breath, and the incoherent screaming until I was sealed in my car or my home. Only then was it safe to dissolve into a puddle.

I didn't think anyone else could-or should have to–handle my full-throttle neediness. Grief and loneliness were my problems to work on. Everyone else had plenty of their own issues. I didn't want them to worry. Truthfully, a part of me buried deep inside believed that if my family, friends, and coworkers cared enough about me, they'd see through my façade, break down my walls, and rescue me from the isolation chamber in which I was living.

It seemed to me that people who fell apart in front of witnesses got lots of sympathy and got rescued in one way or another. I envied and resented those people for getting what they needed, but I could not bring myself to throw a fit in public. I didn't trust that I'd get the same results, and the whole scene would be embarrassing and humiliating for all parties.

Don't get me wrong, I was lucky enough to have the support of a loving family. Well, by the time Doug died, my immediate family had dwindled to one sibling, an older brother who was sympathetic, but I had an unusually good relationship with my small but close family of in-laws. All those people lived far away, though, so I saw them only occasionally. I had a demanding job, so I couldn't go stay with them. Besides, Doug's death was not the only crisis they were dealing with. Another family member nearly lost his life a few short months later, and this young man's recovery and long-term disability required much of their attention.

I had various friends, some of whom reached out and did their best to distract me and keep me company. They provided a brief but welcome respite from the abyss. Being emotionally stunted, however, I couldn't let myself take full advantage of their gestures by being truly needy. I had neglected many long-term friendships over the years or had been content to keep them casual and lighthearted. I hadn't made much effort to develop new friends, because I had my best friend living with me. Doug had provided just about everything I needed for decades. Left suddenly on my own, I didn't feel it was right to dump my problems on my friends. I welcomed spending time with friends, but I often felt out of step with them. I was always focused inward, and my despair and loneliness smacked me in the face all over again the moment we parted company.

Though it was very hard at first to go alone, I made weekend trips to the cabin when I could. I still loved the mountains, but everything along the drive there and everything about the cabin itself reminded me of the happy plans Doug and I had made to enjoy it as a couple. For the first couple of solo weekends, I sat around moaning, "It wasn't supposed to be like this." I also scattered Doug's ashes off the porch where we had envisioned watching hundreds of glorious sunsets holding each other's hand and a drink in our free hands. Eventually I busied myself with furnishing the place; we had just gotten started when Doug fell ill. I found my enthusiasm for the venture slowly coming back as I fixed it up solely to my taste. I loved that cabin and had many good times there over the next decade, but I hardly ever had company to share my enjoyment. I am sad that Doug's vision of sharing good times with good friends there was never fully realized.

Although we lived in different states, my mother-in-law, Shirley, and I were each other's lifelines during the first year after Doug died. My own mother had died of cancer when I was in my early twenties. Shirley had lost the oldest of her three children in a freak accident at about the same time. In fact, Doug and I started out as friendly coworkers who bonded over short discussions about our relatively recent losses, my mother and his brother.

Shirley's grief over Doug's death in 2005 had been compounded by her earlier loss. My father-in-law was a New Englander who handled grief with a stiff upper lip. Shirley turned to me for support and understanding, saying she felt I was the only one she could talk to, that even her closest friends wouldn't understand because they had never lost a child. She felt she didn't belong in a support group like Compassionate Friends because the children she lost were both grown men when they died.

Shirley called to check on me nearly every day for the entire first year, and we cried together, cheered each other up, reminisced about happier times, shared resources on grieving, and helped each other get through every day. I appreciated knowing that someone loved and cared about me enough to keep in close touch when I felt alone in the world, and we both desperately needed someone with whom we could commiserate without censoring ourselves. We didn't stop talking after that year, but we were able to go longer between phone calls.

I decided to sell our three-bedroom suburban Atlanta house and move into a small condo, one of those big decisions that widows generally are advised not to make during the first year. I simply woke up one day knowing that the time was right for me. My job and most of my friends were thirty minutes to an hour away, and I felt I'd be less isolated and more in the mainstream living in the city itself. I was rattling around in the house by myself anyway. Okay, all that information sounds reasonable, and it honestly did turn out to have been a good move for me, but the truth is, selling and moving provided me with a giant project that sucked up all my free time and energy for a good six months. A great distraction! I put real sweat equity into emptying the house we'd shared for eighteen years, dispersing much of the physical evidence of our marriage, but when the hard work was done and I had set up my new city condo to my satisfaction, I realized that I had only put off a lot of the hard work of grieving, rather than bypassing it.

As the first anniversary of Doug's death approached, I found myself slipping to more dangerous depths of the abyss, drinking way too much in my newfound free time, calling in sick to work because many days I just couldn't put on my "mask," crying, crying, and crying, and increasingly desperate to end my misery.

Shortly after Doug's death, I had written a cathartic essay about my frustration in dealing with doctors and hospitals that *Newsweek* magazine published in its "My Turn" column. The article led a friend to introduce me to a woman whose husband was clinging to life in another Atlanta hospital. Through many phone and in-person conversations, I bonded with this woman as we compared notes and I provided moral support. Her ordeal was lengthy. Her husband had suffered severe brain damage, and she had in effect been widowed long before he actually died. We kept each other company, shared macabre humor, commiserated on how rotten a hand life had dealt us, and freely self-medicated our pain. We also debated ways to commit suicide more than once.

It felt so incredibly good to have someone my age to talk to who really could grasp all the many ways in which life had changed irrevocably for me through no choice of my own. I had previously resisted joining an online group of widows I'd come across—part of my subconscious denial that I really was in fact a widow, I suppose—but realizing how valuable kindred spirits were, I immersed myself wholeheartedly in the chat forums of that very supportive group.

I continued to indulge in out-of-control thoughts and behavior, however, including driving too recklessly and drinking heavily, because what the hell, I had nothing to live for. This mindset scared me so badly that I decided to get professional help. No one in my life at that time had ever admitted to seeing a therapist, and my upbringing had led me to believe that a person had to be truly unhinged to warrant it. I figured I probably qualified. I was deeply ashamed, but desperate enough to try it. I was tired of my lonely fight to survive the sinister black abyss.

I got incredibly lucky, because I literally picked a number in the phone book to call, and I found a gem of a therapist I continue to see to this day. I found a variety of other helpful resources along the way, such as workshops, classes, and support groups. All of them shaped who I am today, but none more than my therapist, who laughs and cries with me, champions my growth, and has strengthened my self-confidence immeasurably by helping me figure out who I am now.

Who I am now is definitely different than during the Doug and Diane era. Widowhood forced me well outside my comfort zone, and I cursed this growth while it was painfully incubating, but I am a better person for it, stronger, more confident, more flexible, less naïve, and more self-aware. I've grown to love living alone, and I'm not lonely. As an introvert, I am actually re-energized by solitude. I've dated a little, but I've not yet found my chapter two, but I know I'll be fine if that never does happen though.

I'm more likely to start conversations with strangers now, and I don't shrink from attending events and traveling alone. I've greatly widened my circle of friends who are now mainly single, whether widowed, divorced, or never married. I see and communicate with them way more often than I did while married. Over the last decade, I've built a decent support network, and I'm no longer willing to gnaw off my own arm before asking for help, though doing so is still not easy.

When I retired recently, I made the decision to sell the weekend retreat Doug and I had purchased and buy a more commodious log cabin, so I could make the mountains my permanent home. It was harder than I anticipated to give up the little place Doug and I had pinned our dreams on, but I was exhilarated rather than intimidated by the thought of moving to a small, rural town where I didn't know anyone well. People here are friendly and have a relaxed approach to living that suits me well. I am delighted to have taken up hiking as a hobby at this stage of my life, fulfilling my own dreams of leading an outdoorsy, active lifestyle. I would most likely not be hiking if Doug were still alive, as he was never attracted to it. In fact, I would not have had many of the adventures I've had in the last decade including kayaking and volunteering at the Georgia Aquarium, which led to helping to monitor nesting sea turtles on the coast.

The experience of loving and then losing Doug will stay with me forever, but I have long ago stopped defining myself first and foremost as a widow. It's just one facet of my life now, a life that is very different from what I could ever have imagined, but once again, quite satisfying.

Every now and then I still catch sight of the abyss on the bad days that came careening out of nowhere, striking fear in my heart that I might slip back down to the rim of the yawning pit. But the truth is I will never again allow myself to dwell in that grim place, because now I have the tools I need to stay on higher, more stable ground, and I know where to turn for help when I need it.

6

A Moment in Time

by Diane McMinn

Current Age: 51
Age at the time of loss: 31

In 1982, when I was just eighteen years old, I joined the United States Navy. The ratio of men to women in the Navy at that time was almost two to one. Imagine my joy, when only six months later, I met an amazing man that from the moment I first laid eyes on him, I knew I would marry him one day. Yes, for me, it was love at first sight. I'm happy to say that I turned his head too, because less than two years later, in February 1985, we were married. I was living in heaven on earth. For three and a half years it was just the two of us living, laughing, and loving. Life couldn't have been any better. Wait. Yes, yes, it could have.

In June 1988, I gave birth to our beloved son. Could we be any more blessed? To see the man that I so loved and adored love our child unconditionally and perfectly was almost more than my heart could bear. Again I asked, could we be any more blessed? And yet again, God said yes.

In December 1990, two and a half years later, I gave birth to our darling baby girl. My heart was bursting with pride and joy. She was indeed Daddy's Girl. Our lives were perfect and complete. We had everything we could have asked for; pure happiness, sheer bliss, complete love, it all was ours. I was blessed to be able to be a stay-at-home mom as my husband worked the graveyard shift at our local post office. My children and I had no way of knowing how cruel and horrible life was about to become as our happiness was soon to be stolen from us in an unimaginable way.

Shortly before midnight on October 12, 1995, Pat left to go to work. I was babysitting for our next-door neighbors, at their home, so he walked over to bring our seven-year-old son and four-year-old daughter to me. We said good-bye, and he left without lingering, as he was running late. Since he had left only a little bit later than normal, I remember thinking, "My goodness, he's being a little rough on that truck" as he squealed out of the driveway. I laughed to myself and thought nothing else of it. After all, who was I to question a man and his truck?

Our neighbors returned home at approximately 2:00 a.m., so I left for home. Only then did I realize that Pat had locked all the doors, and I did not have my key with me. As I turned to go back to the neighbor's house, I beeped Pat on his pager over and over and over, but I never received a call back. It was uncharacteristic of him not to call back, as he knew I would never beep him if it weren't an emergency.

Finally, at 7:00 a.m., I took the kids and drove to the post office. I learned that he had never made it to work.

At 9:00 a.m. the police received a call about someone passed out in a vehicle at a flea market about five minutes from our home. They found my husband with multiple gunshot wounds, the fatal one being in his chest. The love of my life and the father of our two beautiful children was dead at only thirty-one years old. I was also thirty-one years old. Pat was taken from us in the prime of his life by a senseless act of violence that to this day twenty years later, remains unsolved.

Twenty years seems like a lifetime. I am now fifty-one years old and have no desire to "move on." I have no desire to "get past this," to plan, or to look forward to a future that does not include him. Besides, I would only sabotage a new relationship with feelings of guilt and negativity. I made plans for a future with Pat, and those plans were destroyed.

I still live my life one day at a time, but that part of me, the part that cared about myself and my need or desire for a man, died with him. To this day I am consumed with anger, sadness, bitterness, hopelessness, and loneliness. My children are the only reason I am still here. Our son was seven years old and our daughter was four years old when their daddy was killed. I remained strong for them because I wasn't going to let the devil win. They had already lost their daddy, and I was determined that they not lose their mommy as well.

They are grown now with children of their own. I have four precious grandsons now and one cherished grand-daughter. My grandbabies are the reason my heart beats, just like my children were and still are. I don't live my life for me any longer and haven't for more than twenty years. I can't get past my loss, I can't get over it, and I can't move on from it. In my heart and in my mind I am still married. I have my memories, and no one can take those from me. I have kept his memory alive to the point that people who have never met him know exactly who he is. My grief is my new normal and will last for the rest of my life. It is the price I will pay for the gift of having him to love. And love him I did, unconditionally and with every ounce of my being. I didn't ask for what happened, I don't wish it on anyone, and I wish it had never happened, but accept it, I will. This is who I am now.

There are good days, bad days, better days, and worse days. Yes, I still live, laugh, and love. I treasure and appreciate friends and family. I have proven how incredibly strong I really am, because my family matters to me more than the next breath I take. I wasn't going to leave my children orphans because I was afraid to live in a world without Pat, but the pain of not having my husband here to go through this life with me will always be present. He didn't just die; he was stolen from us. That kind of grief can't and won't ever be fixed and will always be part of who I am.

I am grateful for the time I did have with him and if the memories are all that I have left, well then, so be it. I just don't have those feelings for anyone else. I never did and I never will, not before him, and certainly not after him. It wouldn't be fair to another man, anyway. It truly wouldn't. I took on the pain of outliving Pat.

I've endured the excruciating hell of not knowing who, what, or why his murder ever happened. I've gotten through the sleepless nights, the tears that wouldn't stop, and the thoughts of wanting to die so we could be together. Why? Because he was mine, if only for a moment in time. And God, what a loving legacy he left us!

7

Test of Faith

by Dayna Bodensteiner

Current age: 44
Age at the time of loss: 41

February 21, 2013, was the worst day of my life. I lost my best friend and soul mate, not to mention father of my children. In the blink of an eye, everything changed. The horrific trauma of that day will be hard to erase, but with God's help as well as support from our family and friends, I do my best to move forward.

I still cannot comprehend how our strong, forty-two-year-old superhero lay lifeless and not breathing. I take comfort in knowing there was no pain. I will never forget being stuffed in that little hospital room where they told us he was gone, but I already knew it in my heart.

My name is Dayna Bodensteiner, and I am a forty-four-year-old mother of three. I started dating my future husband when I was seventeen and a senior in high school. Jon was a big athlete in both football and wrestling with a blue-and-silver mohawk. We were an unlikely pair. I was the student council, band girl, and he was the outgoing athletic star. We went to our senior prom together and then went off to separate colleges.

Somehow we worked through the distance and were married five and a half years later on September 4, 1994, in Rapid City, South Dakota. The pastor who married us was also my cousin, and he gave us some very good advice. He said, "Marriage is like a three-legged stool. You each represent one leg and God is the third leg. Keeping Him in your marriage is essential to your survival." Even though Jon didn't have a huge faith in God when we were first married, we took that message to heart, and our marriage grew stronger with each passing year. We welcomed three beautiful daughters into this world named Sydney, Ashtyn, and Aubrey. We truly lived a fairy tale life until February 21, 2013, when our world would forever be changed.

Jon was a homebuilder who usually left early for work, but on that Thursday, he was working from home on book-keeping. The girls were surprised to see him, but welcomed the opportunity to have breakfast with him. He then drove them to the bus and said, "Have a great day. I love you."

He spent the morning reviewing the books with his brother Adam, who was eleven years younger, but also his business partner. I also usually worked from home, but on that day, I was having a new professional headshot taken. I got all dressed up and headed into town. When I came home, I had the CD of the proofs in hand and found Jon sitting at the computer. I asked him if he wanted to see. He said of course. We looked at the pictures, and he picked his favorite shot. "That one. It's beautiful. No, you're beautiful, and I love you."

I looked up at him and he kissed me on the forehead.

He had his workout clothes on. "I'm going to work out before I meet Adam at the accountant's office," and off he went to the elliptical machine downstairs. I continued working while some time passed. I wasn't sure when his appointment was, so I went down to check on him.

I found him on the floor, blue and not breathing. I initiated CPR but couldn't get any air into his airway. I ran and got my phone, calling 911. The next twenty to twenty-five minutes I continued CPR with the 911 operator on the phone. My nine-year-old daughter came home from the bus and found us, not something a child should ever have to see. I had her go wait for the ambulance and show them where we were. During that entire time, I was sobbing and praying, but I knew he was gone. They pronounced him dead at the hospital, and we later found out he had a massive heart attack, because of a 100% blocked coronary artery.

Growing up in Rapid City, graduating with my future husband, and raising our daughters here, I soon found out the amazing support system my family had in place. Before we even arrived at my parent's house, it was full of friends and family offering their support. Of course social media also played a unique role, notifying the town very quickly. I even think one of our daughters tweeted something from the Emergency Room, which then spread like wildfire.

That very first night after friends and family left, my mind kept replaying all the events of that day, but then rewinding further. We sat in church the night before as a family. We had our personal taxes done the day before, which was much earlier than normal for us. We had lunch with my parents and my sister. We had just celebrated President's Day weekend with some very close friends and commented on how amazing it was. We had celebrated Valentine's Day, and Jon gave me a card that said, "I'm not letting go EVER!" I looked at him confused, because he normally gave me a long sappy Hallmark card. He said, "That's all I have to say this year."

I started thinking back six months and realized we had an exit plan like no other. It started with family pictures the previous summer, continued with a trip to Stockholm to meet my boss and coworkers, a trip to the bottom of the Grand Canyon with his parents and brother, a trip to New York a couple days before Christmas, and a cruise and vacation of a lifetime over New Year's with our girls. It continued right up until the day he died, when he had breakfast with each of his daughters and told them he loved them.

He may not have been aware of his blocked artery, but his soul knew he was leaving and afforded us no regrets. We lived life, but not only that, Jon had business handled and everything in order. It became clear that none of it was coincidence, but instead all part of a plan.

In the days and weeks following Jon's death, we began to see the incredible impact Jon had during his life, which has continued in his death. He was a model father, husband, coach, community member, and most of all a Christian. During those first few weeks after Jon's death, my mother asked me if I was scared. I told her with absolute certainty that I was not. I was devastated and sad, but I had a strong faith that God had a plan for us. I knew it then and still believe it today.

Jon was a strong Christian. We prayed together and he raised his girls with a firm foundation of the bible's teachings. I truly believe the one thing Jon couldn't accomplish while living has been accomplished through his death. His family and some close friends are slowly beginning to see and understand only God and faith can make us whole again. I pray that we all meet Jon again in heaven.

Jon's memorial service had more than 800 people in attendance. The message was based on Joshua 1:9, "Be strong and courageous. Do not be afraid; do not be discouraged, for the LORD your God will be with you wherever you go." We chose that verse because it reflects how Jon lived, and we knew that believing God is always with us was the only way we would successfully navigate our path forward.

People have told my family that we exemplify strength, but I can assure you we don't always feel strong. It is only knowing we are not alone that gives us strength. The pastor also put a twist on WWJD, changing it to What Would Jon Do, as he led by example. This is how he continues to influence people today. We have had many WWJD things made and people carry them every day, telling me stories like, "I went out and played in the snow with my kids today, because that's what Jon would have done." Various athletic teams have put WWJD on uniforms and t-shirts reminding them of how Jon lived. His favorite motto was "Give 110%, ALWAYS!" He was kind, hardworking, cheerful, and respectful, all attributes we try to carry forward in all that we do.

Seven weeks after Jon's heart attack, my mother called me and said, "I had a dream last night. I am about to list a house for sale. In fact I've been working on it for about three months. I've never considered it for you, but last night I saw you in this house. I have been thinking about it this morning and I think it might work."

I said, "Then let's go take a look." The house location was perfect, less than a mile from Aubrey's and Ashtyn's school and about a five-minute drive from the high school that Sydney attended. The owners were in Texas and my mother had the only key. I mention this because as we toured, there was a red mylar heart balloon floating in the living room. My mom said, "How did this get here?"

I told her it was probably from Jon. We both kind of laughed it off and continued our tour, but to this day I do think he was somehow responsible for the balloon's being there. I think it was my first sign from him. I loved the house. I brought Jon's father and my girls to see it over the next couple of days. Buying a new house is a big deal, though, especially when I already owned a very large one. I thought I could secure funds to do so but knew it was a risk to buy before selling mine. On the other hand, I couldn't imagine selling our larger home without a place to go. It seemed like the logical way to do it, if I could financially make it work. Three days after I looked at the new house, I had the approval of Jon's parents, some of his closest friends, and the girls, but I was still afraid. I prayed intensely that night, "God, please help me to know if this is the right choice for us."

The next morning I was alone at the grocery store. I ran into our construction companies' real estate agent, who was also a friend of Jon's, but not someone I knew well. He stopped to talk to me, and I told him all about the house. He listened intently, looked at me, and said, "If you found a house in an area of town you like, with a floor plan you can live with, you need to buy it!" The hair on the back of my neck stood up, and I knew it was my answer.

I made an offer on the house that day. I closed on it June 1 with the goal of moving over the summer so the girls could settle prior to school and getting the old house listed. I never really had to pack boxes. We moved slowly, taking only what we wanted, giving away much, and throwing away the rest. We had the old house ready to list by mid-July.

My mother was the agent and she cautioned me that the price we set was high for the area. It could take a while to sell, which I was financially prepared for. Once again God provided, however, and we had an offer within a few months and a closing by October 1. The people who bought it were from Utah, a retired couple with their widowed daughter, just a couple of years younger than me, who has become a dear friend.

Before Jon died, I did not talk openly about my beliefs or faith unless I was specifically asked. I didn't want to influence others or come across as pushy, because I believe people have a right to their own belief system.

My attitude changed after Jon died. I had two options in dealing with the loss. I could be angry with God and turn away from Him or I could lean on Him. I found a plaque that said, "The Will of God will never take you where the Grace of God will not protect you." I've clung to those words, and it made all the difference for me and my daughters.

I feel more like a disciple than ever before. God has done so many amazing things in our lives during the past three years since Jon died that I cannot keep from sharing them. We found a new church home about a year after his death. The pastor used our story in a sermon series called "Hurt," emphasizing that how you deal with tragedies is a choice. The pastor told me, "God is using you to help other people." His words were hard for me to fathom. Who was I to offer help to others? Opportunities continue to surface, though, and I continue to share my coping mechanism, which has been my foundation of faith and my support system of family and friends.

For the girls, a chapter of a national organization called Young Life has been key to their coping. It is a nondenominational ministry aimed at teenagers. Sydney and Ashtyn had attended local meetings, but after the death of their father, the Young Life leaders became a huge support system for them. They taught my daughters how to lean on God, growing their faith and their relationship with Him. I saw them blossom in their confidence and in how they coped with the tragedy. Today they are Young Life leaders themselves. I've seen them up on stages, professing their beliefs and inspiring others. Sydney once said in front of an audience of 700 people, "We are all going to face trials in our life, and it depends on how you are going to decide to look at it. When I look back at my dad's life, I see him as a role model to me and to so many other people. I see him as a man who lived an amazing forty-two years of life, and so many blessings that have come from his life. There isn't a day that goes by when I don't miss him or think about him, but I get to look back and I see the amazing sixteen years that I had with him. Today I'm okay because I know that God has a will and I will one day get to see my dad again."

I couldn't have been more proud of Sydney, and I have peace that our daughters are going to be okay. Aubrey has also joined in the younger organization called Wyld Life. She attended camp last summer and is starting her journey to grow her faith with some strong role models that we are blessed to have in our lives.

I was forty-one when I became a widow, a word I now despise and that changed the entire course and direction of my life. I had been a team player with my husband for almost twenty-five years. We grew up together, and I planned to continue my adventures with him, traveling the world while raising our daughters. There was no illness, just a sudden moment, and he was gone.

Everything is different today, just three short years later, but not all of it is bad. I know that I am stronger, as are my daughters. There are beautiful sayings about how tragedy can transform you if you let it, and I believe we have done so. I am proud of our strong will and our determination to continue living, in spite of the abrupt and unexpected change in our path.

I am known to take a lot of photos. I love to photo journal trips or events but had no idea I was actually photo journaling Jon's life. In the six months following his death, we sorted through about 70,000 photos. Approximately

500 of them were made into a video that is on YouTube and can be found by searching Remembering Jon Bodensteiner. About 700 of my photos are in a book that we all have. We titled it *In Celebration of Jon's BIG Life!* We found putting these photos together was very healing for us, and when people see them, it is obvious that Jon lived life. We watch the video often, using the memories to bridge the gap until we meet again.

* * *

Dayna continues to write about her life, after the death of her husband, and the signs that God continues to send letting her know she and her daughters are on the right path. She hopes to publish her work in the future. If you'd like to see her story, it can be found here: https://vimeo.com/102666734

Dayna's daughter Ashtyn has created a blog to share her experiences of losing her father as a teenager. It can be found here: https://ashtynschae.wordpress.com/

8

It Takes Two

by Kierra Dann

Current Age: 53
Age at the time of loss: 15

No one ever has been or ever will be the embodiment of my every hope and dream, the fulfillment of every wish, desire, and fantasy, as he was. My every belief was his belief, my every dream, his dream; we were soul mates, meant to be together.

Or so he convinced me, over and over and over.

My dream was of a white dress and to be the woman behind this great man. My dream was to fulfill every aspect of a Christian wife, to be a Proverbs 31 woman.

After a date, he attacked me in my father's living room. I fought, I kicked, I screamed, I bit, I threatened, and I reasoned. All to no avail.

I stopped eating and drinking. I sat in a corner, knees drawn up to my face, sobbing for days. No one noticed. If they did, they didn't care.

I stopped attending school and church. No one noticed. If they did, they didn't care. In the days and weeks and months that followed, I was not shown any care or concern, not offered any comfort, by anyone. Except my attacker.

He flattered me continually. He feigned great remorse and repentance with all the right words. He painted a beautiful word picture of the future we would have, if only I could forgive him, as Christ would. If only I had been more like Christ, the incident would never have happened, he insisted.

Had I been familiar with the Power and Control Wheel, I would have recognized his minimizing, denying, and blaming. I would have recognized the drawing in of the hoovering, the repairs of the make-up mode, and the glow of the classic honeymoon stage. It was all instantly recognizable when I first saw the Power and Control Wheel, many years later.

Through the years the abuse cycle continued, as did the total lack of concern from others. No one noticed. If they did, they didn't care.

I didn't seek out comfort from others. I found that asking, hoping for someone to care, only brought more and deeper pain as I had to face just how worthless and of no account I was considered.

As the pattern repeated, I had sorrow for my lover, so overcome by the demon that was not him. I cared. I didn't seek help for me, but I sought help for him. I bought and read books. I paid counselors.

I continued to believe all things, bear all things, and hope for all things. My love never failed. With each cycle of abuse, he assured me. I felt assured with new knowledge, assured by my fervent prayers, and ever assured by his promises that this time it would be different.

Years passed, babies came, new ploys were adopted. Ten years. Six babies. A new church. A new home.

Life was beautiful half of the time: the honeymooning, the hoovering, and the make-up modes. Of all the trees in the forest, my beloved was the apple tree. What could I do to heal his blight? What was wrong with me? Why couldn't I please him? The children grew. I no longer suffered alone.

My efforts to stop the abuse became more desperate, more adamant, and finally more public.

"What's the matter with you?" "Can't you figure out that behavior isn't normal?" "Why didn't you just leave?" Oh, yes, some people 'cared' enough to ask those questions.

More hurtful than that were the people I expected would show me love. They said to me, "You don't honor him enough," "You don't cook and clean enough," and "You don't understand men."

Never mind there was nothing I wouldn't have given, nothing I wouldn't have done, and nothing within my power I didn't try. Abuse hadn't happened to them in their marriages, so it must be my fault.

How dare they add insult to my injury? May God forgive them and not hold them accountable.

Their husbands do not rape them because they are not rapists. Their husbands do not beat them because they are not violent. They do not continually torment and harass them because they are not sadists. They do not fool them and make fools of them, because they are not liars. Their husbands do not take pleasure in their pain because they are not evil men.

If they were raped, beaten, tormented, harassed, and lied to and about, if they felt hated, rejected, desperate, and alone, I would comfort them. I would protect them.

My deceiver and attacker had the undeserved privilege of being called my husband. He never entered into any covenant. He never loved. He never cherished. He never kept himself only onto me. He never honored. He never protected. He never provided.

He took. He controlled. He overpowered. He was always the one I needed protection from.

That evil men enter falsely into moral and legal contracts should not surprise us. It is little wonder he didn't want to give up my service, my admiration, my devotion, my love, or my desire to do everything and anything, if only he would be pleased, if only he would be healed and whole.

What I was brought to realize is this: He was pleased. He was not seeking recovery from anything. He was living as he chose to live: wielding power and control, using people, and loving objects rather than people.

It never was any different. He never wanted it different. It never would have been different. All the honeymooning, all the hoovering, and all the make-up modes were simply ploys to attain a goal.

Marriage is a mystery, a picture of the relationship between Christ and the church. To call such a relationship as ours a marriage is a mockery of Christ.

The commitment of only one person cannot make a marriage any more than God's love for us makes us partakers of His Spirit, if His love is unrequited.

God will not force Himself on anyone. He does not lie. He does not seek power and control over us. He loves. He gives. We love Him because he first loved us. He didn't pretend to love us because He had a use for us.

A physical act does not consummate a marriage. Two people choosing to love and be loved, choosing to know and be known does. Love and truth are the foundations of marriage. Two people committed to each other.

It takes two.

9

The Disappearing Marriage

by Fred Cliett

Current age: 47
Age at beginning of loss: 35

Summer, 2013

She wakes me with a kiss. It makes sense, because she does it every morning. And just like every morning, it's cold, wet, and sloppy. Her tongue has traversed nearly the entire terrain of my face before I'm conscious and can react. "Jesus, Oreo! It's still dark." A look at the clock tells me she's earlier than usual. "Are you fucking kidding me? It's 4:30."

Even more awake, I'm alert enough to know that any more talking is just going to encourage not only her, but her little brother as well. He's already struggling to work his way out from under a pillow, which is under my leg, which is under another pillow, and everything is under the blanket. Caine is a burrower. He's an expert at finding the maximum amount of bedding and body to crawl under. It doesn't take him more than a few seconds to emerge and join Oreo at my mouth. It's not the threesome any man dreams of, and I push them away, frustrated but careful to keep my wits and settle them down with my best baby talk.

"Okay, guys. Still sleepy time. Lie down. Lie down. That's it." I gently stroke the backs of their heads while pulling them from my face. Just a few seconds is all it takes before Oreo walks in circles—one day I'll research and learn why canines do that—before collapsing on a pillow. Caine takes that cue and begins the five-minute process of burying himself. I'm back in Dreamland before he's finished, and my last thought is that this sleeper/sectional is the best investment I've ever made.

The sofa arrived in 2010, not long after Oreo. Caine joined the slumber party in the summer of 2012. I'd been sleeping upstairs in the bonus room off and on since about 2003, and close to every night starting in 2007. Sometimes I tried the family room sofa or the living room loveseat, and once in a while I'd pass out on the floor of one of the kids' rooms after reading or singing to them while they slipped away into sleep.

Wherever I sought slumber, by 2013, it had been years since I'd slept in bed with my wife; the sectional simply made the bonus room my forever sanctuary. Some nights I would lie next to her, and I might last an hour or two before the snoring drove me out. There was a rock group in the 1990s called The Refreshments, and their song "Blue Collar Suicide" summed it up my situation. The lyrics spoke of a man who couldn't sleep, because his lady snored like a chainsaw. Apparently, she wasn't much of a cook, either. And according to the song, the guy was a writer and she had sucked away all his motivation to put words on paper. He countered all of it by taking pills.

I never self-medicated, but the rest of the song resonated with me.

I'm told marriages can fall apart for a variety of reasons. People split up over money, or more precisely the lack of it. The loss of a child can sure as hell drive a man and woman away from one another, even if neither is to blame. I've had friends tell me, "We just grew apart." I used to want to call that one bullshit. If money is good and everyone is healthy, you should be able to talk things through before the relationship goes bad.

There I was, though, drifting in and out of consciousness in the summer of 2013, knowing that I slept upstairs alone because I long ago gave up trying to sleep next to my wife, but I didn't give up until long after she did.

The snoring used to be cute. It started with the first pregnancy, but it really amped up with the second. While she carried our daughter, she was loud like a rock concert. Yeah, I'm a light sleeper, but she could have woken anybody, and on some nights I didn't have to be in the same room to absorb the sound. Everything we read about it and every doctor told us it was the baby pushing on her small frame. I figured once our daughter arrived and my wife's body took back its baby-free form, the breathing would return to normal and I would return to bed. We laughed about it, especially on nights she managed to snore herself awake. I even wrote a poem describing the racket as a thing of beauty, because it represented not only the reassurance of her presence, but also the fact that she was carrying our child. The next thing I knew, it had been more than a year since our daughter was born, and we were rarely sleeping together by any definition of the phrase.

There's a comfort that comes with waking up next to someone. I rarely go all night without opening my eyes once or twice, so often when I did, I felt the reassurance of having her next to me. No matter what the world had thrown at us, we had each other. The bedroom had long been the place where nothing could get to us. The bills, the insanity of our extended family, home repairs; nothing was allowed to harass us once we turned in for the night. It was an agreement between us that was never discussed but was always there from the beginning. In the daytime we talked openly about our workdays and worries, but bedtime was our time. If we weren't having sex or sleeping, we made plans for the weekend until one of us couldn't stay awake any longer.

We shared everything there was to share in that bed, and as gradual as the process may have been, we lost everything when I stopped spending time there. One day I woke up and recognized the absurdity of our situation. How could two people who never fought or even raised their voices come to a point where they rarely fell asleep together? Why did we stop making plans? The magic went out of the bedroom in every way.

All her life, she struggled with her weight. She's never been morbidly obese, but she's barely four feet, eleven inches and carries too much weight for someone so short. Neither of us should have been surprised when the snoring all but disappeared when she started to shed pounds in 2007. She was beginning to feel better about herself, and we were fooling around more than we had in years. By chance, I fell asleep before she did one night, and before the snoring got to me. I woke up with the sunrise and could barely hear her breathing. *I just woke up in a real bed, next to my wife. She's losing weight. She feels good about her body. We're having sex. She's not snoring.*

Later that day, I couldn't shut up about it. I told her she looked great. I told her the night before had rocked my world. I told her that she didn't snore. And I told her that more important than any of it, I loved waking up next to her. Whatever she needed to continue down that road, I was on board with her. I would eat what she ate. I would even cook it. I would exercise with her. I wanted to wake up with her every day for the rest of our lives.

Two weeks. It lasted two weeks. I can't remember what derailed it. Maybe she had a bad day at work, or she might have just wanted some comfort food one night after eating clean for so many days, but the carbs came back, then the weight, then the snoring. It didn't matter that I kept offering my culinary services and my encouragement. One night she even said, "It's too much work. I'd rather *enjoy* dinner, anyway."

Now it's 2013, and the dogs are licking my face awake. Six years ago, I thought she and I had recaptured something lost, and we had done just that, for two weeks. It was a great two weeks, but now it's been a long six years. It's been an even longer six months, because I've tried every way I can think of to express my thoughts on all of it. She's tried every way she can think of to tell me it's all part of the deal, and when both kids are gone in seven years, we'll work on getting it all back.

I've already waited that long. I'm not doing it again. I'm going to fight. I'm going to come at her with everything, and I'm going to do it in the nicest way possible. I'm going to set up date nights. I'm going to cook the right foods. I'm going to go out for walks with her. I'm going to do everything I can around the house, and I'm going to make sure the kids are ready for bed on time every night. I'm going to do it all in such a spectacular fashion that she won't be able to say no to me when I give her a suggestive look. We're going to have amazing sex and I'll pass out from the ecstasy. On the nights we don't, I'm going to smile and tell her I'm tired, too, and I'm going to go to bed with soft music on my headphones and hope to fall asleep and be deep in R.E.M. before the chainsaw hits its peak. If I'm doing everything right, the chainsaw is going to go quiet soon enough, anyway.

January 2014

I don't know why she said no. It was winter break, the kids spent a night with her parents, and both of us had some time off. At a park on a gorgeous lake just a few minutes from our house, there was an art display, sculptures with lights that looked nice during the day but amazing at night. I wanted to take her to the park, walk around the lake, and enjoy the show. Perfect weather, perfect night, perfect date. I don't know why she said no, but she suggested relaxing on the couch with a movie. I started the movie. She opened her laptop.

Summer 2014

I know I want to leave. I'm having a hard time expressing it to her. I've told her I'm not happy and that something has to change. I've told her I don't care that everyone else goes through the same things, and I've told her we've never been everyone else. We've never fought about money. We've rarely fought at all, and we've always fought fair. We're better than everyone else, and sometimes other couples tell us we are. But they don't know there's trouble in paradise. I tell her it's no way to live for the next six years, and I tell her we'll have nothing to go back to once both kids are gone. She tells me it's life.

Fall 2014

We're falling apart. She's finally figuring it out. She knows I'm miserable. I know she's starting to get scared, but it's incredible how she's holding on to her beliefs. *People just deal with it. Did you think we'd be infatuated forever? Did you think we'd always be nineteen and not able to keep our hands off each other?*

I tell her that I never expected to be teenagers forever, but it would be nice to share a bed and share our bodies once or twice a week. She asks me when I stopped being attracted to her, which seems ridiculous to me, because she was just saying we weren't meant to be infatuated forever. I tell her than even if I had stopped wanting her, she stopped wanting me first. It's like a kindergarten squabble; we're both more concerned with who started it than making it right.

December 2014

I'm looking around my apartment. It's only a two-bedroom. When the kids come over, my daughter will have her own room, and my son can sleep in mine. I'll stay on the couch when they're here. It's not perfect, but it's going to have to do for now. A lot of things are just going to have to do.

What amazes me is that I'm not really amazed. It's been such a long path to get here that it makes a lot of sense. There was no other way for it to end. The kids have been good about everything. My wife is a different story. She's crushed. I'm trying to be decent about that, but at the same time, I don't get it. Things happened over the course of some years, not just a few weeks or month. For the longest time, we were business partners. She says I'm shallow to leave if it's only because I was no longer attracted to her. She tells me she'd be fine with it if I just came back, continued to live upstairs, and went out whenever I wanted. I try for the hundredth time to explain that's what got us to this place, and she tells me I'm destroying my relationship with the kids. She explains that she meant it when she stood in a church and took me for life. I respond that she hasn't been to church in years. She then tells me she's been praying every night since I moved out. I've never known her to pray; I don't think she prayed even when we used to go to church. I don't think she prayed *in* church. While neither of us is perfect, I know I tried to fix it, and I know she didn't think it was broken. We each have our story, and those stories are too different for us to work it out.

Summer 2015

I worry about bills. I worry about making my rent each month. She worries about the kids, but I don't. Again, they're doing great. I feel a sense of loss, yeah. I never expected to be forty-seven and single. I don't hurt, I wish only that I had moved out sooner, so I'd be further in the process. I don't want to be alone the rest of my life. I don't want to be alone at all. I lost the ideal and the part of the American dream that included a house and a family, but I've got a roof over my head, and I've got the love of the two greatest kids I could have hoped for. I lost a few years, years I could have and should have been happy. I can't recover the years, but I can be happy again.

10

A Hairball With Teeth

by Alora Gilman

Current age: 44
Age at the time of loss: 33

"It wasn't viable with life; it couldn't have survived. It was basically a hairball with teeth," the doctor explained to us much more buoyantly than I would've expected.

As I fought to control the tumble of emotions rolling through me, I watched the doctor steadily to determine why he was speaking in such a lively manner. Was it relief? Joy? Was he having an aha moment? It seemed he was all three.

I'd been under the doctor's care for the past year after trying to get pregnant for a year before I met him. Eight weeks prior to today he prescribed birth control pills to minimize the size of an ovarian cyst. He didn't know I was two weeks pregnant, so I suppose he was relieved and happy he had definitive proof that the birth control pills couldn't have caused the miscarriage.

Tissue from the dilation and curettage procedure had been examined and found to contain sixty-nine chromosomes. Healthy fetal tissue should contain only forty-six chromosomes after conception, twenty-three from the sperm and twenty-three from the egg. In my case, two sperm had entered the ovum late in its life cycle when its protective wall was weakening; therefore, forty-six male chromosomes battled to link one-to-one with twenty-three female chromosomes. They couldn't. The twenty-three-twenty-three double helix ladder that is supposed to be created by an equal number of chromosomes could never form. My miscarriage followed.

Let's back up two years. That's when we had started trying to have a baby. After the first six months I was in disbelief that it wasn't happening. Conceiving easily was an assumption I took for granted. I'd had no reproductive issues, no abnormal results on any annual exam. I was young, thirty-one, and the picture of health. No women in my family had ever had fertility issues.

A year later we met with a fertility specialist who conducted the usual barrage of tests. The results showed there was nothing wrong with either of us and there was no medical reason why we weren't able to conceive. The news was more disappointing than if there'd been an issue. An issue can be fixed.

The self-pity, anger, and frustration of being unable to conceive was all encompassing. I could focus on nothing else, and it affected every facet of my life. It's true that when you really want something, it's all you see. I swear every other car on the road had a Baby on Board sign. Babies were in every aisle at the grocery story, in line at the pharmacy, and at the table next to us in every restaurant. I stopped looking at babies.

I'd hear news stories of child abuse, neglect, or death at their parents' hands, and I'd become infuriated. How could they be blessed with child after child only to harm them? Why couldn't I, who would not harm a child, have one?

If one more person told me I wasn't getting pregnant because I was stressed out, I was going to pull the person's hair out. Women all over the world lived in famine, amid disease, or in fear of their lives daily. Somehow they were still getting pregnant. My stress level living in the United States with my comfortable life? Not even close.

I felt like I was being punished.

Nearly two years after all of our fertility attempts started, I was put back on birth control. Six weeks later I took a pregnancy test, because I wasn't getting my cycle. I was pregnant.

My doctor was surprised and said he had no way of knowing I was pregnant when he had prescribed birth control. I went in for the first ultrasound at eight weeks, and we heard the heartbeat. Two weeks later I miscarried. That's when I was told "It was basically a hairball with teeth." It broke my heart. No, it broke my soul. If I couldn't get pregnant and have a baby, fine. I'll figure out how to deal with it. But don't give me one just to take it away.

I had no idea that losing a fetus that wasn't even fully formed could be so painful emotionally. It wasn't like I'd lost a baby I'd held in my arms. I never would have understood the devastation had it not happened to me. The only time I'd ever heard of someone having a miscarriage, the girl was in high school or college, and she wasn't exactly sad.

I was destroyed and deeply depressed by my loss. I didn't want to tell anyone, because I honestly felt I was being punished for being a bad person. If I dared to share the news, I expected the people I told would also think I was being punished.

For about three months after the D and C, I isolated and comforted myself with food–lots of food. I cared less and less for my appearance. I wore the same clothes over and over because I didn't feel like going to the dry cleaner or doing laundry. I approached everything with apathy and disregard.

Slowly the black cloud lifted and I had more happy days than sad days. I can't say why, other than it just took time. I looked at my wonderful husband and thought, "Even if we never have a child, at least I have him." I was back to my old self about six months after the miscarriage. I even forgave the doctor for his incredibly tactless method of delivering the news to us.

I started telling others what happened and was surprised to hear how many friends had suffered a miscarriage or their sister had or their best friend had. Sometimes I heard about multiple miscarriages. It seemed it was more common to have one than not to have one.

I did eventually give birth to an adorable, healthy baby, for whom I thank God every day. I also gained an understanding of the crushing emotional pain involved with a miscarriage, something I would never have grasped, had it not happened to me.

11

Gift of Love

by Deborah Hope

Current age: 64
Age at the time of loss: 59

I never knew a cat quite like Kordell. He was lively, fun, and often acted more like my third son than a pet. He was an unexpected gift from my oldest son, Michael. A nuclear tech in the Navy, he adopted Kordell and introduced us to him.

Jim, my husband, shook his head at Michael the way he often did when our boy did something without thinking. "You will be going out to sea. The Navy doesn't allow cats aboard a ship."

Michael gave us his confident smirk. "Don't worry, Dad." He patted Jim's shoulder. "I'll find a good home for him."

A week later, Kordell was living with us. The six-month-old was not a happy kitty, especially after we had him neutered and declawed a month later. He moped around the house, eyeballing us like we were the reason he was miserable. I felt bad, but knew he'd be better off with those operations. I comforted him with a stroke of a hand, a mother's voice, and the occasional bits of fresh turkey from the dinner table. Soon Jim, Kordell, and I became a family.

One time when Michael came home on leave to visit us, he said, "Where's my cat?"

I waggled a finger at him. "You're not getting Kordell back. He's our son now."

For the next nine and half years, Kordell, Jim, and I lived in South Florida. Kordell was at home in our quaint Lauderhill house. His favorite spot was our screened-in porch. When he wasn't stretching his long orange and white body over the porch floor sunning himself, he chased lizards and bugs. He signaled he was ready to come back inside with a paw on the sliding glass door and an expectant look on his face. Inside, he was the king of his castle. He strutted around like a police officer working his beat, making stops at his food, water, and kitty litter.

In the evening he lay on his preferred dining room chair, tucked under the table. From his hidden perch, he'd spy on visitors and keep his nose alert for the dinnertime snacks that Jim twitched at every time I sneaked Kordell a sliver of chicken, bacon, or turkey, his personal favorite.

Kordell was very loving. Whenever I got his brush out, he'd run to me and start purring. He loved to be brushed, arching his back and giving his kitty smile every time I did. On days I was not feeling well, he jumped up on the couch and lay by my side, as if he knew.

After Jim retired, we moved to Tennessee. I wasn't sure how Kordell would handle the move, but our Florida vet told us as long as the cat was with us, he would be fine. We packed up with Kordell at our side, and off to Tennessee we went.

I watched Kordell closely when we arrived. His feet touched the floor as if he wasn't sure of the slick surface. We'd always had carpeting, but now we had hardwood floors. When Kordell worked up the courage to investigate the new house at a trot, he went sliding. I laughed but felt bad for him. In time he got used to how the floors felt and walked the entire house with more confidence, although I could tell he liked our bedroom best. It was carpeted.

When my son John and his family visited us from Florida, his oldest, Jaina, found my floor pillow in my bedroom. I sometimes used it for my back when I watched television. She decided to put Kordell's favorite blanket on top of the floor pillow. Kordell saw his blanket and lay on top of it and the floor pillow. I knew I'd never be able to use the pillow for myself again.

As the years went by, Kordell aged and started having medical problems. When he reached fifteen years old, our Tennessee vet told us it was time to have him put down, for there wasn't anything more they could do. On May 3, 2011, we said good-bye to our loving Kordell.

Even now, years later, when I think of Kordell I get teary-eyed. It's hard not having him here with us.

This is my last farewell for Kordell. We will always love him and miss him. Kordell was a gift from our son Michael, and Kordell became our third son. A gift of love.

Good-bye, Kordell.

12

The California Jug

by Donna Parrey

Current age: 65
Age at the time of loss: 4 – 19

A large glass jug, topped with a cork, sat in the corner of the parlor floor, not too close to the heat vent. Scotch-taped to the side of the jug was a worn white paper label on which my mom had printed Disneyland, but it was always referred to as the California Jug. It was made of amber glass that brought to mind the suntanned happiness and carefree joy I associated with the prospect of my entire family visiting California one day. We saved pennies, nickels, dimes, and the occasional quarter in that jug. Each clink of a coin brought us closer to our dream vacation.

In the 1950s, California seemed like the other side of the world to our New Jersey family of six, but it was our goal to load up Dad, Mom, and four kids spanning thirteen years in our red-and-white station wagon and drive from Trenton all the way across the USA to the gates of

Disneyland. Mickey, Minnie, Goofy, Donald, and Pluto would be there to greet us. The promotions we saw on *The Mickey Mouse Club* promised us that whirling rides, singing and dancing shows, and more awaited us.

Every few months I'd glance over to check the level of coins in the California Jug. Sometimes it appeared never to move, but over the years, the level climbed from just a few inches to nearly a foot high. Some part of me truly believed that when the jug was full, we would go.

In the meantime, our family spent many Sunday afternoons exploring attractions nestled in the back roads of New Jersey and Pennsylvania. Gingerbread Castle, The Land of Make Believe, and Jenny Jump Mountain were just a few of the visits that kept us kids happy and our family together. Faded photographs from those days defined how blessed we were. Even when we had no particular destination in mind, we'd pile in the station wagon and just go for a ride, singing endless harmonizing rounds of "You Are My Sunshine." We summered at the Jersey shore in a tiny, salty bungalow, jumping the waves and collecting clamshells, all of us getting as brown as the California Jug.

I don't remember exactly when we let go of the dream. My older brother got married. My sister and I got jobs. My younger brother got a dog, but our family never got to California. I often wondered if my parents felt disappointed or if they were like me, happy just to have had a shared dream over the years.

Decades have passed. Dad and Mom are gone. Some of us kids have grandchildren. Some of us live in Florida. All of us have experienced multiple visits to Orlando's Disney

World, Tampa's Busch Gardens, and other major entertainment complexes that have sprung up. Oompah bands and the chorus to "It's a Small World" are the soundtracks of those excursions, yet none of it can compare to the long-ago thrill of hearing the clink, clink, clink when I dropped three more pennies in the California Jug.

13

Missing the Meaning of Meat

by Stephanie Marinos Boda

Current age: 58
Age at the time of loss: 50

I am a fifty-eight-year-old Greek woman, which indicates that I was once a little Greek girl. This fact also indicates that my life has been centered on food, Greek food: good food, festive, colorful, and highly scented. Garlic, oregano, lemon, and olive oil fumigated my parent's kitchen as did the smell of Ivory soap on the washcloth that washed the lamb grease off my chubby round face. Generations of cuisine passed down from foreign islands and unknown ancestors gave me an identity that I never realized went much deeper than the buttered layers of baklava.

An unpredicted turn in our family's lifestyle has left a gap in my identity that has transported me to a new land, one in which the ancients would find lacking. I do as well.

My first memory of food, and a distinction that my lunch box presented from that of my peers, was when I was in first grade. My dear Greek mother would pack my school sack with the best cream cheese and olive sandwiches on Hollywood Diet Bread along with Greek cookies, while my friends washed down peanut butter and jelly with boxed cafeteria milk.

My mom was known in the community for her "spanikopeta" or Greek spinach pie, as the Americans called it. Her recipe originated from a particular part of the Greek islands and it was always a huge hit with Greeks and non-Greeks alike. As a child I watched her gentle strokes as she brushed and buttered each layer of paper-thin phyllo dough into the pan, layering as gingerly as a designer meticulously layers wallpaper. She topped the dough with the tastiest combination of spinach, feta cheese, cottage cheese, and eggs and then covered the treasure with added layers of sheer floured sheets. The results sprang out of the oven as a crispy, buttered spinach and cheese pie that delighted every sense and was swiftly devoured by anyone within reach. Spanikopeta was only one of the many that structured my identity, first as a Greek who loved food and then as a Greek mother who loved to cook the dish for my own family and friends.

My heritage and those meals that expressed a deep part of who I am naturally progressed into all I enjoyed serving as a homemaker. I found extreme joy that Mediterranean food was not only fully enjoyable to most palettes, but was also often toted as a healthy food plan, and through the years I felt the freedom of sharing this cuisine at parties and holiday events. I never realized how much my womanhood as a Greek cook was wrapped up in the dozens of rice and lamb grape leaves that have been rolled and steamed on the stove, until a grave change occurred in our family.

A few years ago, when I was in my mid-fifties, and going through menopause, I may add, three of my children became vegetarians. One developed celiac disease and two sons became gluten intolerant. The vegetarian diet was manageable for the most part, as our Mediterranean lifestyle includes eating tons of greens and could be converted to meatless options easily enough. So I thought.

The gluten problem was more difficult to adhere to and created tremendous stress as we watched one child rapidly lose weight and his strength. It was quite a dilemma as to what to cook for the no-meat crew and the no-wheat kids.

As time went on, my vegetarian children developed a deeper conviction concerning eating any animal products and progressed to adopting a full vegan lifestyle. Out went the spinach pie and cheese, at least Yiayia's recipe. Not only did several of the authentic Greek daily dishes need major renovations, so did the bulk of my holiday meals, including Dad's favorite Christmas tenderloin.

For the first few months or so, I rolled along pretty well in the unknown territory of extra beans and rice. I didn't object to having several tofu meals as the guests requested either, for we were saving money on the grocery bill for our large family. I tried to cheerfully adapt my thinking without too much stress and strain, but as the vegans tightened the reigns and the options lessened for the gluten intolerant, my cooking experience went from delightful to dreadful. Eventually I snapped.

The loss of familiarity of what I had always known and took such pleasure in was gone. The planning, shopping, preparing, eating, and serving slammed me with an emptiness that became all encompassing. It created a loss that caught me quite off guard. Not only was my womanhood affected, but also my motherhood and a large part of my heritage as well. My childhood became disconnected from me, and my artistry as a cook felt stripped away. The reality of the depth of loss in not knowing what to cook was shocking to my life, and though I logically tried to embrace the change as positive growth, my being was bruised and beaten up. I became angry at my children, at food, and at my own attachment to resistance.

My time at the grocery store became a sour experience. Shopping for food used to seem like a field trip, as I stationed myself in front of the imported cheese display and transported my thoughts to France or Italy. The grocery list became severely limited as I tried to convert the family to a more vegan/gluten-free way of eating. Shopping for the variations of palates was confusing and became increasingly overwhelming as I threw out more meat for just the potatoes. I found myself lamenting at Safeway's chicken counter as I reminisced about the weekly tradition of Greek avagolemono soup with Challah bread, a blessed union of Jewish and gentile fare.

What about Greek Easter? How in the world could I wrap my mind around the fact that for the majority of our household, the Greek cookies that Dad and the girls would make would have to be nixed. And the lamb? Surely lamb could be eaten if only once a year for the holiday.

Greek children not eating lamb, isn't that sacrilegious? I tried to be optimistic about cooking the lamb separately, but the ingredients taste best in the lamb zummi, cooked all together.

The loss became greater and greater as more native foods became heads on a chopping block. Adding brown rice to every meal was not a satisfying substitute, and my creativity that once was expressed in croissants and eggs Benedict with hollandaise sauce evolved into several celebrations of emptiness and boxed cereal. I felt betrayed like when I received a box of sticks from Santa one Christmas.

The family thought I was making too much out of the shift in meals, and my dear husband couldn't understand why I couldn't just toss cold cuts and gouda in the shopping cart at Trader Joe's. Why not just slip the forbidden into the fridge and call it a day? If my emotions were only that simple. If only my cultural identity, my female hormones, and my creative expression could be fulfilled by tortillas and salsa.

I would love to proclaim that I gracefully sauntered into the new lifestyle alternative, but I did not. Food felt like an enemy at times, and the ambience of my kitchen went from a place of welcoming to a war zone. I abandoned my stove. I even abandoned the grocery stores. My confession of pain appeared to be diminished among new recipes of curry soup and one more tofu stir-fry. Holidays were stressful and dry, and soon the topic became gravel in my mouth. Some of those special days have been thrown out, leaving me feeling shallow and superficial.

Time does have an interesting dimension, and its passing can often diminish a debilitating sting. My food crisis has lessened its clutch on my life over the past several years, and I have grown to guiltlessly garnish my Greek salad with salmon and feta cheese again, without trying to prove that the goat was milked humanely and the fish was caught by hand. I have also learned that I cannot be all cooks to every kettle. I now let most of my adult children prepare vegan recipes for the whole lot of us. I've relaxed when my husband flings beef raviolis into the shopping bag, and I unapologetically continue to buy whipping cream for my morning coffee.

I do not begrudge my family anymore for their eating restrictions, whether self-induced or doctor prescribed. The new awareness of animal cruelty and factory farming that my children have educated me on has actually benefitted my life and encouraged me to think more holistically. Having a greater understanding of celiac has increased my compassion for others with serious food allergies. This food crisis has in many ways forced me to make lemonade out of lemons, but the foundation has permanently changed. The smells, textures, and tastes are different, for the most part, and although I am free to eat anything, the gap is still there. The loss is the event. The dream was the experience.

The experience of forming ingredients into delectable designs brought me back to my parents' pantry, my mother's soft hands dipping Greek doughnuts in a mixture of hot honey and crushed walnuts, and my father's strong arms beating the beef and barley into a tasty, salty mush. All these sensory scenes made me Greek and gave me my identity as a woman. I miss the days of festive fancies when I coordinated the ham perfectly timed with the cream cheese mashed potatoes.

Those days are no more. The new recipes are different, and I am adjusting, for man does not live on bread alone, and surely my identity isn't entirely wrapped up in Greek meatballs. The absence of all those delightful dishes renders the table food a little less delectable, but we have learned as a family to unite over salad and seaweed, and I have come to realize at my age that even in my losses, I have much to gain.

14

It's Now

Anonymous

Current age: 36
Age at the time of loss: 25

I was always an inquisitive child, and that trait bled over into my early adulthood as well, it seemed. Our annual family vacation had started. As we waited for the others to arrive in the following days, I sat alone with my mom enjoying the sand, the sun, the peacefulness of the waves, and the solace of her uninterrupted company. "Mom, tell me, what has been the best part of your life so far, and what has been the hardest?" Already anticipating her answer, I mentally went on to my follow-up question sort of half listening, half taking in the scenery.

She answered what the best part of her life had been so far, and to this day I have no recollection of what she said. What I do remember hearing is, "It's now. The hardest time of my life is right now."

I stared at her blankly. This answer wasn't at all what I had expected. And like a sniper's bullet, I knew instantly something had hit me, but the confusion of from what direction it was fired, and the fleeting last seconds when I was ignorant of the degree of the injury, were upon me.

We were the textbook southern family. We called our parents Mama and Daddy, even as adults, and our relationship with them reflected that sort of sweet adoration of each of them. They were fine Christian folks, active in the church, and intent on having us learn the truth of our faith and apply it in our lives. My parents had the best group of friends, constantly traveling, boating, eating out, and doing life with the greatest group surrounding them.

As a family unit, we were close. Both my parents told us kids on many occasions about the way they struggled in the beginning of their marriage, the way they pulled together to mend their differences, and the gratitude they had for all they had been blessed with as a result. As we children were approaching and were well into adulthood, we were enjoying our parents now as friends, as grandparents, and as role models in business and in life. They had lost everything early in their marriage as the result of a poor financial arrangement in a new business. From nothing they reinvented their life and their business to become wealthy. There were many reasons to admire them, but the lens that I saw them through was still ultimately as their child.

"Mom, what is wrong? What is going on? What...?" The questions kept coming, never pausing for answer, as I sprang forward in my beach chair.

"Well, her name is Misty."

As the next hours unfolded, my mom walked me through the early findings of my father's betrayal. The details she shared that day would only scratch the surface of the grotesque revelations of deceit in the months to follow. Many of those months it felt as though I was in some sort of alternate universe from which I was soon to wake or be freed from. My dad left us for a drug-addicted prostitute? He was teaching Sunday school last week and we had family dinner three days ago. How could I reconcile these truths? I still can't.

What I do know is there was no good resource for adult children of divorce. If you were a child under twelve, my God, there were 84 million strategies abounding on how best to transition into this new phase. "Mommy and Daddy love you. We will always be a family, but we are going to live in separate houses with swimming pools and new puppies." When you are twenty-five, though, you meet a girlfriend to drink wine every night, go to work the next day and pray no one asks why you look so tired, and date a few dirt bags that will treat you as badly as you think you deserve, to match the shit you feel inside. You question everything about your life. Was everything a lie? Were they pretending the whole time I was growing up? What part of my childhood was authentic?

The childhood I described before was virtually wrapped in yellow crime tape and set on fire. The "friends" my parents had? They scattered like ashes in the wind. Most were quick to join the church leadership and judge my dad and cast him aside. Apparently thirty-five years of morality won't earn you the right to being treated like a human being when you fail miserably, at least not if you're a Baptist.

Precious metals withstood the fire. They were the few friends of my folks that I saw in public, and as our eyes met, they saw my shame staring back at them. Shame not because I did something wrong, but because I was the offspring of the person that let us both down. Those precious metals walked across the room and treated me as what I was, an adult child, but no less a child. They hugged me and said, "I called your dad this week. It was great to hear his voice." Those are the precious metals that gave me permission to feel, feel what I needed to feel, which was permission to love my parent despite his shortcomings.

Perhaps when parents divorce after the kids have left the nest there is an assumption that the parents had put in their time. Because of our chronological age, some parents submit us to being their mediator, sounding board, secret keeper, and the list goes on. It's the worst kind of abuse. You can't be my hero and my project. You will have to forfeit a role. I am begging you still to always choose the former.

Lost dreams. On each and every Christmas Eve, you will find me overdoing the occasion to distract myself from the reality that it was always my family of origin's most special evening. Without exception, you will find me at some point in that evening reapplying mascara and drinking too much wine, because the pain of what that night should be is too much to bear. My kids should be driving my parents crazy somewhere as I finish playing Santa. Those days are gone.

I grew up believing I was the center of my dad's world. For twenty-five years that fact was my gospel. While I sat on the beach that afternoon, my self-worth washed away with the tide. If my dad didn't love me enough to stay with my mom, I had overestimated my place in his world. Those days were gone.

I grew up in the church with the belief that those precious people in the congregation would love me and support my family always. Ego and politics plague human nature. My confidence in God is still alive, but my identification with "His flock" proved unauthentic. Those days are gone.

Always and *never* are words I no longer use or believe in, as they relate to human behavior. Nothing is for sure, even from those we hold the closest. Those days are gone.

Someone wise once said, "There are moments that mark your life, moments when you realize nothing will ever be the same, and time is divided into two parts—before those moments, and after them."

That summer day on the beach marked the end of "before."

"After" is still unfolding. I would like to believe that I have gained something from the same pain that took so much from me. I am, without question, a more empathetic person. I have a heart for those who have messed up, because I know firsthand that fabulous people can make equally terrible mistakes. I know that I have a perspective on parenting that I would not have had, had I borne my children during the "before" age. I know concretely and without exception that I am a parent for life. I am not a parent until my children are eighteen. They will always look to me as an example, even as imperfect as I am. I do recognize what they will still need from me as adults. That understanding influences my choices daily.

The pain of loss will never hurt less. That's the biggest lie of loss. You just find a way to live or function in the pain. Today I love my life. I love my husband, my children, and my friends, and I don't walk around with my pain raw and exposed, consuming me as it once did. But the sight of a grandfather cheering at his grandchild's game, seeing my mom sit alone in church, or trying to coordinate three Thanksgiving meals to accommodate all of the brokenness can send me spiraling down into the pit of the pain. Our family home and our time as an unbroken unit seems like a foggy dream to me now, a part of life that I loved but can't spend too much time recalling without feeling the loss overcome me. I am determined to make the "after" as meaningful as the "before."

I accept that it will never be the same.

I accept that those dreams are lost.

I accept that those days are gone.

I anticipate the rest of the story with eagerness.

I can be found in any one of those four sentences at any given moment, but I try to move more quickly through the first three and keep striving for the last.

Gratitude is the key that frees me from the prison of the past. For all that has been lost, there is much that remains. For all of the lost dreams, there are many that have been realized. This is where I choose to sit today, in the present, taking stock of all that I have, rather than dwelling on what is gone. Beauty for ashes.

15

The Story of Josh

by Jules Zurich

Current age: 67
Age at the time of loss: 35

Fearful trepidation beleaguers me as I approach the structure. It towers over me, and as before it dares me to make the ascent. Wedging my feet and hands between the grime-coated planks, I painstakingly start the precarious climb, one slated frame after the other. After I manage ten, maybe twelve steps, panic and agitation fill me, tempered only by an unrelenting determination to conquer the imposing beast. I cry out in an attempt to overcome my acrophobic fear. "Damn you, let me cross. You must let me cross." My cries are followed by a blood-curdling scream that emerges from the depths of my vocal cords.

"Wake up! You're having a nightmare again," my wife grumbled, nudging me in an attempt to rouse me from my slumber.

I shouted out again, something incomplete and incomprehensible, rolled over, and found myself sitting on the edge of the bed, suddenly awake. My blinking eyes squinted to impede the undimmed light from my digital clock displaying 5:15 a.m. Deserting me to deal with the terror on my own, my wife rolled over and fell back to sleep. I was wide awake, taking in and expelling heavy breaths to calm myself, angered by the ridiculous recurring nightmare. Sleep was pointless, so I arose to start the day early.

By the time I rid myself of morning breath and made coffee, it was 5:45 a.m. A Tuesday, it was another typical weekday, except I had been awakened an hour before my usual time. After pouring myself a cup of coffee, I draped a blanket around my body and retreated to the cool open air of my patio. This time of day was still my favorite, a carryover from the days when I lived in my utopian world with the Intracoastal Waterway for my backyard. Life seemed less complicated then, for I prided myself as being a worldly man; liberated, self-reliant, impenitent, and unconcerned with the trials of others. In those days it must have been benign self-indulgence that kept the impending nightmares at bay.

The nightmare insidiously slipped back into my mind. Suppressing it, I diverted my thoughts to the present and considered how much life had changed since the days of secluded living by the water's edge. With the unpleasant dream stored away, I relaxed in the comfort of my woven lounge chair, enjoying the counterfeit representation of my previous Shangri-La. The circulating water lapped at the swimming pool's edge instead of a craggy rockbound

seawall. Looking at a natural mangrove's bounty, repro-
duced by a carefully planned landscape and manicured
weekly to maintain perfection, I sipped my coffee, thinking
ahead to the day and the week, thinking about life. A perfect
time for reflection. The house was quiet. My wife and two
children were still sleeping. They would be up soon getting
ready for school in the usual haphazard way, running to
and fro, trying to gather their books, clothes, and lunch,
and the day would be in full swing.

The daily grind with its responsibilities and chores were
welcome, for they neutralized those distasteful memories of
the past. This morning was one when I reexamined my life,
though, wondering how the recurring nightmare would
play out if I overcame the towering obstacle in my dream.
What would happen if I actually made it to the top and
then found my way to the other side? What would I find?
With the years gone by there had been plenty of time to
consider the implication. I already knew the answer, but
my self-imposed forbearance suppressed the complicity.

I had been married to the same woman for slightly
more than nine years. Only two years after our marriage,
the first of our girls was born. Two years later our second
daughter came into being, not exactly planned, but God
decided to bless us in ways that only He knows. The two
beautiful baby girls, perfect clones of their mother and
father, represented the ultimate example of the culmina-
tion of the love that my wife and I shared. I was thankful
for my family, knowing that it was their love that separated
me from my earlier narcissistic ways, yet it was that same

love that brought me closer to face the towering stumbling block in my insidious nightmare.

That particular Tuesday I was looking forward to the evening, the Halloween celebration at our church. Unlike the secular world, our family celebrated Halloween differently. The kids, even some adults, dressed up, not in scary costumes, but in happy outfits, not to frighten, but to inspire or to honor those who God selected to proclaim His name. The church's back lot filled with games, with candy and prizes as the rewards. Even the youth pastor let himself be the victim in the dunking tank. Of course there was the hayride. How the children loved the hayride!

The Halloween celebration was everything it was touted; fun for all, adults included. The kids ran from game to game, the longest line being at the "dunk the youth pastor." Every kid gave it a try to hit the bull's-eye to release the latch that held the pastor in his chair above the water tank. Funny how the latch remained in the stuck position most of the night. I'm sure Josh would have hit it with full force on the first try and gleefully dunked the victim. After all, a father should teach his son how to throw a ball with speed and unerring accuracy.

The hayride was on every kid's to-do list. Each time the tractor pulled up with its trailer filled with hay, the youngsters were like groupies at a rock concert, rushing to jump on board. After some necessary crowd control, I watched as my girls finally made it on board, tentatively gripping the wooden side rails. The tractor lurched into gear and drove off into the night, entering the enchanted darkness of the church's expansive treed property. Both my daughters looked back with fearful delight as they bounced along, but I knew that if Josh were with them, he would have held their hands and calmed their nerves. A wise dad instructs his son to shelter and console the females in his life, even if the ghosts and goblins are imaginary.

With the week behind us, the weekend activity was on tap. Considering fall was upon us in north Florida, Saturday could very well be the season's last day at the beach. We arrived early and found the perfect spot. The girls wasted no time in grabbing their buckets and shovels, running to the water's edge, and beginning the process of building a city of sand castles. My wife and I spread the blankets, poked a hole in the sand to insert the umbrella, and set up the beach chairs. My chair was one of those special inventions you might see on late-night TV, with a wide range of comfort adjustments, headrest, and cup holders galore. Settling in to the calming cadence of the ocean, I dozed off as my wife kept a keen eye on the kids.

My inner consciousness relayed a message of distress as heavy eyelids fell into sleep, but it was too late. It started again, the unrelenting invasion of my mind, always when I least expected it. It began as before. I approached the structure once again as it towered over me, daring me to take another step, except this time it wavered as I pushed on it. The massive frame listed backwards, so I pushed harder, forcing it to lean even farther, allowing for a scalable ascent. Ignoring the filth and grit, I clambered to the top and looked beyond. A charcoal gray mist swirled before me, stretching far and wide. Wondering what was concealed in its depths, I reached out, grasping at the nothingness.

I heard the voice, quiet, yet clear as a whistle, "Daddy, Daddy, I'm here. I'm right here."

When I awoke from the dream, my eyes grappled with the brightness, unsure if I was lucid or incoherent. The light was sharp and clear, though, so luminous that I thought a divine light had penetrated the veil that separates heaven from earth. It was just an instant, but I thought I saw him bathed in the brilliance. He was sitting with my daughters, making sand castles, and like any older brother with his siblings, he boasted his adolescent superiority by making his towers bigger and better. In the blink of an eye the vision was gone.

For years fleeting visions continued to ambush me, ever since that fateful day twelve years before, a day that lurked in my memory, emerging as it haunted me whenever I saw a father with his son. I missed my son, and I longed to see him, to hold him, to protect him, to bring him to the age of consent, to teach him how to be a man.

The love for my daughters is no less than that for my son, but girls are inherently feminine. I like them that way, all the lacy dresses, the Barbie dolls, the makeup, the frou frou, the giggling silliness that makes them so perfect as females. Someday they will shake loose the adolescence and grow to become women, ultimately seeking a mate. Therein lies the reason why boys should become men, as no real man is complete without the love of a woman. Indeed, the mystery of monogamous devotion may come with duties and responsibilities, but the paternal influence instills the confidence for a son to accept the challenge and take charge of his own life. I am not privileged to bring my son to manhood, though, not privileged to be the father who would teach chivalry, masculinity, integrity, and those things that turn a boy into a bold, virtuous, God-fearing man. I forfeited that right with my selfish actions.

A few weeks went by, and I was once again troubled by the dream. This time it was not sleep that allowed my thoughts to be governed, but the words of a wiser man, a man whose influence shaped my life in more ways than I can count. Many would call the man's words incendiary or even delusional; however, he was recruited by the highest power to speak words that originated from ancient times, times when men were not concerned with the distraction or pressures of a materialistic world, or worse, given over to the self-indulgent views of a secular society.

I had chosen to dwell in secular society while filtering out the chicanery spewed by the progressive pundits, but his words overrode the rhetoric, and they found me. This wiser man of influence went straight to the heart of the matter. He talked of life and death in terms that I had rejected, not because I did not accept the truth, but because I had been resistant to confront the truth. They penetrated my conscience, deeper than ever before. His words resonated with such powerful effect they slashed away layers of denial and pierced my heart. He spoke of pain that could be heard. He spoke of helplessness because there was no one to provide relief. He decried those who did not advocate and preserve life. He denounced those that carried out an agenda that advocated death. He vividly described how victims had no voice, no way to defend themselves, no way to cry out or beg for mercy.

And so that terrible day of twelve years ago is upon me. It has been living in my dreams for what seems to be an eternity. Deep set emotions well up from within as memories seize my current state of mind. Conceding to my nightmare, I approach the structure and apprehensively stand before it. This time it does not defy me. Instead it wavers and begins to draw down. I no longer have to climb its verticality, for it has become recumbent, allowing unimpeded access. My trepidation is so intense I am almost debilitated, but resistance is futile, as I am drawn slowly across the bridge, crossing from my present reality to an uncharted mysterious realm. Peering into a murkiness that offers no substance, no physical matter or material, a surreal universe abducts me. It is too late. There is no way to turn and run from what I am about to relive. I drift aimlessly; the reticent darkness surrounds me, and the memory floods my mind.

"This won't take long," a woman's voice assures me through the murkiness.

Turning to the voice I see only dusky shadows. Another female voice speaks from a different direction. "I am very sorry to tell you this, but we have a problem."

"What kind of problem?" I hear a voice respond in the gloom before I realize it's my own voice.

"Apparently she has complications from colitis. We can't risk a procedure here. She has to be taken to the hospital."

A flashback materializes in the darkness: they wheel her through the lobby on a gurney as I dispassionately watch. A look of terrible fear is on her face. I try to speak to her, but she turns her head away from me. A moment later she has been whisked away by the ambulance.

"What just happened?" I ask myself, suddenly finding myself in a compacted universe filled with men and women rushing around in white or green attire, their feet, heads, and mouths covered with linen-like material. What should have been a simple procedure has turned into an emergency. My mind, like the awful ghoulish world that refuses to release me, has become muddled. Confusion and despair sweep over me. Confidence and fortitude have been replaced by doubt and weakness. An imperceptible spec of virtue pings me, because I know I have a chance to reverse my decision, to make things right. Instead I'm guided by selfishness, my self-indulgence overriding moral and logical reasoning. Through the darkness of this illusory universe another voice reaches out. "How will you be settling this? Check or credit card?"

Our relationship had ended weeks before. A sense of relief comforted me when I thought we were finally finished, but my deliverance was short lived when she came one day to tell me she was pregnant. Disenfranchised by the shocking reality, I groped for acquittal. I was faced with the hard choice: check or credit card, life or death? Dispassionately I made the choice and presented my payment to settle the bill, and in doing so I sealed my son's fate. He would die on the operating table. He wouldn't even see the light of day. His life would end in the womb, a womb that God created for the nurturing and protection of a child, a womb that had become no better a place than the gas chambers of Auschwitz. The chamber had become my son's place of death.

I watched the scene unfold as if I were viewing a ragged 1920 silent movie clip. I paid the bill and walked out of the hospital without looking back, knowing she regarded me with hatred. Returning to my temporal waterside sanctuary, I dismissed the day's events as an unfortunate yet necessary maneuver to re-simplify my life. I had washed my hands of the whole affair, thinking that it ended there.

Instead it had only begun.

With my nightmare complete, I struggled to leave behind my personal hell, crossing the bridge back to everyday life. As the gloom disappeared behind me, he cried out to me again like he has done so many times in my dreams, "Daddy, why did you kill me?" His words would haunt me for the rest of my life.

I am aware a day of reckoning has stalked me for twelve years, and today is that day. Why today? Why did I come to church this particular day? Why did this wiser man have to preach about the awful truth of abortion? His words crushed my selfish barriers, dismantled the worldly arguments advocating choice.

He brought me to the brink of that infernal bridge residing in my dreams; he lowered it and forced me to walk across it into the pitch-black depths of perdition. I understand why the darkness existed, because the stark truth would be displayed in its purity, as a raging fire burns against the blackness of the night sky.

Today this man's words convicted me of the most barbarous sin I will ever commit. His words brought me to my knees, and the floodgate opened. The hour of reckoning descended upon me with a fury I couldn't even imagine. I had lost loved ones before, but I had never been stricken with such grief, such disgust. Had it not been for my wife's comforting hands and compassion, I would have lost all control. I was driven by supreme guilt. My self-loathing pushed me to the edge of depravity, a place so vile, so sinful that I had less than the moral equivalency of a venomous snake. I had become the perpetrator, the accuser, the judge, the jury, and the executioner all rolled into one. In essence, I had murdered my own son. Indeed, I didn't stab him with a needle or forcibly crush his head with forceps, but I was the one who gave the command, the one who paid someone else to rip apart Josh's helpless body, to be discarded with the daily trash.

* * *

It has been sixteen years since my day of reckoning. Today my two daughters are grown; old enough to drive, drink, vote, get married, and make their own babies. From the time they were old enough to enter kindergarten, they asked me on more than one occasion, "Dad, are you sure you don't have a long-lost son out there?" They always wanted a brother, like so many of their friends had, and they never let me forget it.

Such a cryptic question. If only I could tell them, "Yes, you have a brother, but your brother is dead, murdered by the man he should have trusted more than anyone." The fantasies of old would resurface, my girls playing games with their brother, digging in the sand, riding on the hayride, and sharing endless other activities. I would have delighted in those moments.

Of course if I told my daughters the truth, they would ask why, and I would tell them. I was driven by narcissism. I was under the delusion that the child would have been inconvenient. In retrospect, sure, it would have been inconvenient for a while, but I would have adjusted just as we all do with children. Josh was a gift from God. If I had opened it and accepted it with the spirit it was given, I would have a living, breathing son, and I would have been a better man.

How do I know I had a son? I don't know, but deep inside I am convinced my unborn child was the boy that I always wanted, so I named him Joshua and gave him life, even though he could exist only in my mind. He will always be Joshua, affectionately known as Josh. He will always be with me until I die, and then, if God grants my prayer, we will be united in heaven. That dream is my only true hope for redemption.

This account has been written with a purpose. It's not to seek redemption by man or by God or make an attempt to rise above my sin or to give myself value for the awareness of my transgression. God knows I have begged for forgiveness and I know He forgives those who repent. I consider myself fortunate because I do have God and wonder how others deal with the grief if they don't have a spiritual connection. Repentance does not make my situation any easier. It does not solve my intrinsic human emotion of guilt. I live with the horror of my decision every day, so I have told my story because I am a man. Knowing that many women deal with the guilt and trauma of an abortion, it's important to remember that each pregnancy started with a man. If a man is any kind of man at all, especially one who has been saved by the blood of Jesus Christ, then he will suffer as much as I have.

As for the woman who was pushed into having the abortion, our relationship was indicative of the consequences when two people are filled with carnal greed. The ultimate price for desires of the flesh was paid for by the life of an innocent unborn child. Selfishly I admit that I hope never to see her again, but if I do, I will ask for her forgiveness and hope she can find it in her heart to forgive me.

More importantly, if I have the privilege to know Josh in the next life, I pray that he will forgive me for what I have done.

16

The Dream of a Child

by Joan Coonprom

Current Age: 57
Age at the time of loss: 40

The smell of a newborn after a bath, the baby's first smile, a child's dimpled hands, and uninhibited belly laughter are little things that bring a smile to a mother's face as she envisions them. Many of us dream of having children one day.

We married later in life. I was thirty. He was thirty-eight. We anticipated a life with children, but were not specific about our timeline and assumed parenthood would happen naturally at some point. We were not concerned the first five years. We were busy adjusting and settling into married life, but as I passed my thirty-sixth, thirty-seventh, thirty-eighth, and then thirty-ninth year without a child, we grew increasingly anxious.

As I approached forty, we finally pursued fertility testing to see if a biological cause could be found and corrected. A test revealed that both my fallopian tubes were obstructed. Scarring and adhesions resulting from infection and peritonitis that occurred when my appendix ruptured at age five was the likely reason.

In the recovery room after the test was over, I received the news that without considerable intervention and even then, with no guarantee of success, it was impossible for us to conceive a child. My heart constricted and I felt as though I had received a fist in the stomach as the reality of the news sank in. Tears flowed from my eyes as my soul howled. During times of extreme grief and loss, I do not sob or weep on the outside; I leak. The pain is so intense and so gut wrenching, it has to find a way out. Unconsciously, unmindfully, the tears just run.

Activity and busyness have always been my way of coping. I got up the next morning and got busy, and then the headache came. It was extreme migraine-level pain, and nothing I did relieved it. A call to the doctor and subsequent conversation with the anesthesiologist revealed I was suffering from a spinal headache from the spinal anesthesia administered before the procedure at the hospital the previous day.

As the fluid leaked at the base of my spine, my brain stopped floating and settled onto the base of my skull, producing a headache of prodigious magnitude. The risk of getting a headache of this type is one in one hundred to one in five hundred procedures. I was instructed to lie *flat on my back* for three days to give the puncture an opportunity to heal, which would relieve the pressure on my brain. Keeping busy to avoid the specter that had come into my life was not an option. I was required to lie flat on my back as the wraith of the bad news hovered over and taunted me. My mind began an unhappy recital.

The child we had dreamed of was not a possibility. There would be no bath times, no chubby dimpled hands to touch my face. We would never hear the belly laughter of our child or see Mommy's eyes or Daddy's nose. We would grow old alone. We would never have children or grandchildren. Eventually one of us would die, leaving the other utterly, wholly, and completely alone. I realize that foster care and adoption were possible, but my mind was not willing to go there at that time.

As this oppressive spirit taunted me and my mind continued its relentless negativity, the happiness, hope, and joy for life drained out of my soul. I felt I was being sucked down, surrounded, and oppressed by sadness and hopelessness. I couldn't see my way forward. I had to find a way out or continue falling into despair. I needed someone or something to reach down and pull me out.

In my desperation, I reached out for a book from my bedside bookshelf. My books double as journals and are like old friends. We exchange ideas as we converse and interact. I read and put notes in the margins and highlight what resonates with me. When I pick them up and reread them, I can see how a passage influenced me at another time. Sometimes it will be a new passage from the book the strikes a chord with me. Sometimes the same passage resonates in a different way. We develop a relationship over time. I love my books.

I picked up a devotional book titled *God's Best for My Life*, by Dr. Lloyd John Ogilvie. I was at the threshold of a new era in my life, the dawning of life with a new reality, however negative. I needed thoughts appropriate to a new beginning. I needed something to inspire, to breathe life into my soul. As I lay on my back, I read the entry for January 1. The key verse was Jeremiah 29:11 (RSV). "For I know the plans I have for you, says the Lord, plans for good and not for evil, to give you a future and a hope." In his reflections on this verse, Dr. Ogilvie talks about believing "more in future than in the past" and that we must believe that God has good plans for our future. We need to have hope. Hope empowers and gives us confidence and courage and vision for the future. Dr. Ogilvie says, "The gift of hope for the future is the key entrusted to us which opens the floodgates of the Lord's power and unlocks the flow of His amazing, unlimited possibilities". God is in control. He has a plan. He wants us to become more like Him. Put your trust and hope in Him. Dr. Ogilvie closed the devotional with a thought for the day: "God's best for my life begins with a vibrant hope for the future." In response to what I had read, I wrote the following prayer in the book:

7/10/98 Lord, I need that vibrant hope today. I am discouraged and feeling hopeless. I'm trying to trust the future to You and that You have a plan in all of this, but it's hard for me to see now. If this is planned to help me become like You, please teach me quickly. This valley is very dark and I need Your light to see what's ahead.

The Lord answered that prayer and did bring me hope and strength, not as a lightning bolt, but slowly, incrementally. God often uses the most unlikely messengers (Balaam's ass in the book of Numbers comes to mind) and the most unconventional methods of delivery.

After the required three days of bed rest, my spinal leak healed and I was able to get up and go out to the backyard, sit in the sunshine, and play with a litter of kittens that were a godsend for me at that time. They were just old enough to romp and be playful. Their pogo-stick bouncing antics, pouncing on each other and rolling into a ball, rearing on hind feet and swinging their chubby arms in the air were a great source of joy that was balm for my soul. The spirit that had oppressed and taunted me began to lose strength and dissipate. Seemingly insignificant moments of time become etched in our memory. Sitting in the sunshine, watching and playing with those kittens, brought me joy. Their enthusiasm for life brought me hope. They were not concerned about the future at all. They were fully in that moment enjoying life. Oddly enough, they enabled me to do the same thing.

Postcript:

The remainder of that year was a time of growth, learning to trust, walking by faith, and having hope. Six months later on New Year's Eve found me in front of the fireplace with Dr. Ogilvie's book, again reading the devotion for January 1. Here is what I wrote. I actually had to tape an extra page in the book!

1/1/99 No mind has conceived what God has prepared for those who love Him." 1 Corinthians 2:9. I read through this devotion just after midnight. I have also just read through what I had written in July when I was in bed recovering from a spinal headache and being told we would never have children.

I'm now in my fourth month of pregnancy, and I am filled with hope and anticipation. You are a great and awesome and powerful God. You truly do turn our sorrow into joy.

I'm hard pressed to find words that can capture the contrast of feelings between that day and today. I would not have dared even to dream that I could become pregnant, but You say, "I know the plans I have for you, plans for good and not for evil, to give you a future and a hope." You have restored unto me that vibrant hope. You have brought me out of that dark valley by the light of Your love and filled me with excitement and anticipation. You are a God of amazing, unlimited possibilities. Even our doctors have had to acknowledge Your hand in this, as they have been unable to provide a medical explanation...My heart is filled to overflowing in a way it has not been for a long time. It's full of praise, wonder, love, amazement, awe, gratitude, and anticipation. I praise You for Your patience and faithfulness.

The details of how my pregnancy came to pass, other than the obvious, and the outcome represent a story for another time. I will just say that our child was conceived without any medical intervention and was born healthy and normal on the day before my forty-first birthday. He is the best birthday gift I have ever received!

What I want to leave you with is how God and my faith in Him brought me through a dark and difficult time. My belief is that He is able to do the same for you. When we are in the depths of despair, it is hard to have enough light to take the next step, let alone imagine we will feel joy again, but the light can come again. Joy can come again. Do not lose hope. Do not lose a sense of humor. Sometimes answers may come in the way we had hoped for, and sometimes God will bring answers in a way we did not anticipate. Just trust that He is able. I will not say that walking that walk will be easy. Just take one slow step at a time, in faith. Look for joy and humor in the moment. There will be those who come alongside to help us if we take a step and reach out. God is not limited in the tools He has at His disposal. In my case, He used a book and a litter of kittens to bring joy and hope and to start me on my journey.

"He settles the childless woman in her home as a happy mother of children. Praise the Lord."
—Psalm 113:9 NIV

17

Learning to Kick

by Arielle Haughee

Current age: 32
Age at the time of loss: 28

*Student names have been changed for confidentiality purposes.

December

"You're stepping on my boot," *Jason whispered/ yelled to the kid in front of him. Oh, that child!

Get on stage and do what you're supposed to do, I told him with my eyes. We'd been practicing for two weeks straight, and I wanted our efforts to show. The line of elves in their jingle-bell hats was adorable, even though they were fifth graders, a little too old for cutesy plays, but that year was the last one they'd be able to do it before they were thrown into the world of middle school.

*Miguel gave me the sweet smile he'd started to shine my way ever since he broke down and told me about his dad's life sentence. I sat with him all afternoon that day and let the rest of the class read quietly, so he could open up to someone who would listen and truly care. And here he was, saying his lines perfectly in that silly cartoon voice, the boy who used to knock over desks and tear up his work. I was proud of him.

A line of shoes appeared on the cobbler's workbench as the elves marched off stage singing. Little *Marie, dressed in all black, stayed crouched beneath the fabric-covered table. She took her job very seriously, reprimanding any child who messed with her props during rehearsal, a dedicated student, even in the hours we spent together after school working on her reading. Never complaining, she read a passage over and over to fully understand it. I wish I had her tenacity.

Raucous applause followed the end of the play, mostly coming from other students. Not many parents came to these things in this kind of school. It didn't matter, though. The kids all crowded on stage and took exaggerated bows, repeatedly. Their faces were bright and merry, just like the holiday season. I hoped they would take their feelings of joy home with them over the break, no matter what kind of situation they called home.

"I'm so glad you did this," a fourth grade teacher said to me as the students cleaned up. "Really gives my kids something to look forward to next year."

Even though this year was my seventh teaching, the thought of another school year always excited me. I loved the freshness of it all; new decorations, new kids, and new challenges. My smiles were endless the first two weeks of school when the entire year was full of dreams. My husband refused to check the bank account at that time, but just shook his head at all the bags of supplies piling up in our office. I would go into the same spiel about under-privileged children, poor school funding, and the need for hands-on learning. He could probably say the argument for me verbatim. At least he understood and supported me in my career. It wasn't about the money I took home, but about making a difference in the lives of children. It was my gift that I could give the world, and I loved it.

Every year I got better, honed my craft. I pictured my classroom in three years, when all my thematic units would be assembled, all my materials collected, all my students getting where they needed to go. I was almost there, almost to my dream of the perfect classroom. I needed just a few more years of work to get it.

While hugging each child on the way out, I noticed *Simon standing in the corner, pulling the caps off my dry erase markers. He knew how much of a stink I made about keeping them closed tightly, because they were expensive to replace. I took a deep breath and walked over to him. "What's going on over here?"

He replied with a series of angry grumbles, a muffled curse word or two hidden in there.

I knew his tactic. He was delaying having to go home for break, back to a very unstable situation that tore him apart inside. I'd be upset too.

Carefully tugging the markers out of his hand, I set them on a nearby desk and pulled him into my arms. "I'm going to miss you. Now you better say you're going to miss me too, or I'll put you last in the lunch line for the rest of the year."

He snorted a small laugh. There's my boy.

I pulled back and gave him a kiss on the forehead, an act that could easily cost me my job. Go ahead and fire me for giving love to a kid who needed it. I'd do it again, every time. "I'll see you again very soon. Okay?"

He gave me a tight hug before joining his friends in the hallway.

I couldn't help the tear that escaped. I always cried when my babies left. At least it was winter break, and I wasn't the blubbering mess that came with the end of the school year. I had more time left.

A week later, Tim and I sat swallowed up in the couch I bought years before with my very first paycheck. The carnage from our frantic gift opening was evidenced by the crumpled paper lying all over our living room floor.

"We have got to get to this room," I said, sipping my Riesling. We'd been in the house for less than a year, our marriage somehow still surviving the tens of fix-it-up projects we'd put upon ourselves when we signed the paperwork for the place.

"I'd really like to get that surround sound set up in here."

I chuckled. Of course he would think of electronics first, not the walls or curtains or any other decorative item. Everyone has priorities. Tim put his arm around me, and

I leaned into him, enjoying the time with him the winter break afforded me.

Perhaps I enjoyed it a bit too much.

January

"That's a plus sign."

It was 2:00 a.m, and I felt the call of nature. The directions on the box said to take the test first thing in the morning. We'd decided this bathroom break counted as first thing.

"The line is so light." My voice was a fragile whisper of its usual tone. "That can't be right."

"I think you're pregnant, sweetheart."

Tim put his arms around me, and I gripped his shoulders, my mind a small boat on a churning ocean, crashing around listlessly. I wanted more time teaching. I wanted my house to be in order. I wasn't ready for a baby yet. Why did it happen to me? My boat was breaking apart, sending me flying into the frigid water.

June

For the next few months I floated, drifting on the surface, my belly growing more and more round, my mind not fully able to grasp the impending change.

"What is this thing?" Tim asked, holding up a box of lab equipment.

"That's a large screen microscope. I was going to use it for a plant unit one year. I just hadn't gotten to it yet."

"I see that," Tim said as he ran his fingers over the unbroken seal. "How much did we spend on this thing?"

"Just stick it in one of the science boxes."

After deciding I would stay home with the baby for a while, we had to pack up all my classroom materials. I didn't realize how much I invested in my work until it was all stacked in a growing pile in front of me, seven years of memories, of ideas, of plans, all tucked away into neatly labeled boxes.

"Do we really need to keep all this stuff?" I knew he was picturing our tiny attic and maneuvering all those boxes in the cramped, sweltering space.

"Yes. I'm going to need it when I go back, eventually, and I can use this stuff with Luke when he gets older."

I went over to my chapter book sets and began loading them into a plastic tub. I needed to keep my hands busy. My heart was already aching from saying good-bye to my class earlier in the day and managing the mixed emotions they had about their summer break. What would happen when they came back for Meet the Teacher with their younger siblings next year and I wasn't there? I had been the stable force in their lives for a full year, and I would be gone. No one at work knew I wasn't coming back, a necessary evil to keep my health insurance. I was lucky my classroom was on the end of the building where we could sneak the boxes out to our cars like foxes slinking away with eggs from the henhouse.

When I grabbed a stack of copies of *Bridge to Terabithia*, a small piece of paper slipped out and floated to the floor. My eyes watered when I read *"I love you, Mrs. Haughee. You're the best! Love, *Miguel."* What if there was another boy just like him next year who needed me?

A tear fell down my cheek, and then another.

Tim wrapped his arms around me.

"I'm abandoning them."

"No you're not. You've done so much for your kids over the years. And you'll be back." He ran his hands up and down my arms. "Just think about how much you love your students. You'll love your baby even more."

A deep sigh escaped my chest as I mulled over this thought.

"Just picture the first time you see him, right there in the hospital, when they hand him to you."

An image formed in my mind, a clean room, a smiling nurse coming to me with a sweet baby wrapped in a blanket. I could see his tiny face. "Olive skin and dark hair, lots of dark hair."

"Of course you think he'll look like you." Tim laughed. "Now think of how much you'll love that little baby, right from the start."

I'll run my hand over the soft hair and look into his dark eyes. I'll feel it instantly, that maternal connection that every woman in the history of our species feels when she first meets her child. The abundance of love will overwhelm me.

"You're right." I released myself from his embrace and set the note in the box with the rest of the books.

The loving connection I felt with my students would just shift to my son, still propping me up in the water. I would keep floating on my journey. I wouldn't let the stirring waters pull me down.

September

Thunder boomed outside and the lights went out in the hospital room. For just a moment darkness surrounded us, Tim holding one leg, the nurse the other.

The power clicked back on, and the obstetrician gave a nervous laugh. "Almost there. Keep pushing."

Tim's jaw dropped when the baby's head appeared, followed quickly by the rest of his little body.

A tiny bundle was brought to my arms. He was pink. He was bald. He was screaming and covered in fluids. Where was my olive-toned little angel with the dark hair? I looked at the little baby and didn't know if it was truly mine. Where was that rush of love I was supposed to feel, those first precious moments when we feel the binding rope of love tie around us forever? All I felt was confused. Things weren't what I expected. There was no warmth surrounding me. Instead I felt coldness creep under my skin, water beginning to lap over my face.

November

"Come on, Luke," I begged my two-month old as I bounced him up and down in front of the stove, the vent blasting white noise behind us. I'd already tried the swing, music, the rocking chair, and our now patented "shake walk." Nothing was working that day. Forty more minutes until he could eat. The doctor told us we had to make him wait or we would aggravate his reflux, making him spit up. It didn't seem to matter what we did, he spit up all the time anyway. And cried. He cried and cried constantly. What kind of mother was I that I couldn't get my baby to stop crying?

I was completely submerged, sinking further and further each day.

We needed to get out of the house. Bouncing him wasn't working.

Stepping into the backyard, I began my usual circuit around the pool, bouncing up and down along the way. Luke's cries died down to the occasional whimper. Thank the Lord, I could hear my own thoughts. All I needed to do was walk around the pool for the next thirty-five minutes, and I could enjoy the tranquility and be outside the house, the cage that trapped me every day and held me in limbo.

At least we had gotten around to landscaping the yard. We couldn't have that jungle in the back with a kid around. My feet were relatively clean from all my walking, not coated in grime that wedged between my toes like when I did playground duty.

A hardness expanded in my throat, reaching into my chest to grip my heart. What time was it? Would I have been outside with my class now?

I kept walking, knowing that if I stopped, the baby would fuss immediately. "Don't think about it," I said aloud, forcing the tightness to abate. You were supposed to talk to your baby. I never knew what to say. This was as good as anything else.

Not thinking was my strategy. I didn't think when I went to the store and saw the school supply displays. I didn't think when I saw all my teacher friends share news from their classes on social media. I didn't think when one of my previous students sent me a message online. I didn't even read it. I couldn't, or I would live the truth that I wasn't there for him anymore.

When Tim came home at night, he would take Luke to give me a break. What was I supposed to do with no baby? I wandered the house aimlessly or sat down in agitated unrest. It didn't matter what I did with myself. The next day would be the same. Nurse the baby, soothe his fussing, clean the spit-up. Nurse, soothe, clean. Over and over. My life had become a gray carousel, turning at a maddeningly slow pace.

I lay in bed looking up at the ceiling and thought, *Is this it? Is this all my day was?* I closed my eyes and refused to think, just let my mind bounce around, finding no purchase within me.

February

I used to run. I could run for miles and miles, hours and hours. Sometimes I hit a point where my legs felt as if they weren't part of my body, but deadened tissue that had turned to lead. Moving them required immense strength and the belief that they were in fact still attached, even though they felt like metal weights. Still I ran. I kept going, pushing and pushing until I got where I wanted to go.

Every particle in my body had turned to lead now, sinking me deeper and deeper into the blackness below. This time there was no stopping point. There was no bottom to hit. I just continued on my way down, the pressure tightening around me.

It had been months of the same day. No weekends, no vacations, no holidays. Every day was baby day. I became a nesting doll. Opening me up would reveal layers and layers of the same thing inside, but empty of anything else. I could no longer keep my mind empty. I had to face what I'd become. I wasn't doing anything for the world. How was it an improvement to go from working with twenty-five children to just one, and doing a piss-poor job of that? My teaching materials sat unused in the attic, collecting dust, just as I was. How did I feel so connected to my students, but not to my own son? Why did every other new mom seem to be blissfully happy and have the perfect little baby?

I'm not sure what I thought motherhood was going to be like, but it wasn't what I had. Luke deserved a better mother than me, one who was more patient and happy at home. I messed up, did something wrong somewhere along the way; probably did everything wrong. Maybe if I were a better mother, he wouldn't cry so much. Maybe I wasn't really the loving person I thought I was.

I didn't know how to fix things between us, I just knew that neither of us was happy. I needed to do something for us both to bring some brightness into our days.

On one of our daily outings, we were walking around the hardware store, taking our time in the ceiling fan section. Luke could watch the lights and spinning all day. I never bought anything when we visited and wondered if the store clerks would eventually tell me not to come back.

"There's your favorite, Luke." I pointed to the fan with the lantern-style lights. When I turned the corner, a bright display caught my attention. I approached rows and rows of seed packets, each promising a cheerful bounty to bring light into my days.

Everything I needed was right there: soil, seed trays, a watering can. Visions of a yard layered with blooming flowers flitted around in my head. I would lie in the green grass next to a bed of smiling petunias and the sun would shine down on me, warming me, breaking me free from the coldness that had become my constant companion. I grabbed seed packets almost madly, as if a timer were about to cut me off.

"We can set these trays up in the sunroom, little Boo," I said as if you could call the cheap shed-like attachment to our house a sunroom. The wide windows would give ample sun for the seedlings, though.

Hurrying home, I put Luke down for his nap so I could start my new project, the lifesaver we desperately needed.

March

Tiny green shoots stretched out of the soil, turning their faces up to greet the sun, trays and trays of them, covering the floor of the sunroom. They kept me from sinking further, holding me still in the water, as if the seedlings laced together to form a net around me.

Luke and I went out there every day, watering them and giving them the best care possible. Often I would plop his vibrating seat out there and sit down next to him, just looking at the seedlings, swearing I could see them grow.

Luke was out there with Tim, mesmerized by his daddy's bubble blowing, while I folded laundry inside. A crash echoed through the house, quickly followed by glass shattering on the floor. My skin prickled when I heard the baby crying. Racing across the house, I dashed into the sunroom. The baby lay on the floor, broken glass all around him.

Snatching Luke up and giving him a quick once-over, I turned to my husband. "What happened?"

I noticed a four-inch gash across Tim's wrist. His skin flapped down to reveal the inner parts of his arm.

"I leaned on the window, and my arm just went through it," he said, staring at his arm in disbelief.

Had he hit a vein? I couldn't tell.

I dialed 911, and soon rescue personnel swarmed the house. I could barely hear them over Luke's crying. They hauled Tim away in an ambulance, leaving me behind to figure out what to do.

After a trip to the hospital, some good news, and several stitches, we were back home.

The next few days passed in a blur, me bouncing back and forth between taking care of the baby and helping Tim.

Naturally I didn't realize what I was neglecting.

Sliding open the sunroom door a few days later, I glimpsed the wreckage inside. Glass shards were sprayed around in a glimmering display by the window. A barren wasteland stretched out across the rest of the room. The soil dried up so much it shrank into little squares, as if the walls of each tray were suddenly electrified and the dirt became too afraid to touch it. My precious little seedlings were shriveled crusts of what they once were, barely noticeable, laying flat atop the brown soil.

I slumped to the floor.

The seedlings were just beginning to taste life and had much more to grow, to give, to shine into the world. Because of me, though, they were lying flat on their dirt graves. I had let them down.

The water poured into my lungs as I submerged into total blackness. The pressure crushed me like an empty can. My leaden body continued downward into nothingness. I needed to stop sinking. Now.

Where was the girl who could run forever?

She was still there, somewhere. I had to find her.

I had to kick, kick my deadened legs, kick until a fire raged in my muscles, pushing and pushing myself upward. My happiness was something I needed to fight for, every day. Luke deserved a better mother, and it would be me. If I could work with kids in poverty and get them to read and solve math problems and care about school, I could do motherhood. I needed to find the core of determination hidden inside me and pull myself up, breathe the fresh air above. My motherhood adventure hadn't turned out the way I thought it would. I lost myself somewhere along the way. I'd find me again, and this time I would be even better. I started to kick.

Three years later

"Quit laughing at him and encouraging it." I can't help but laugh myself. In front of me is a baby smearing red and blue finger paint all over his face and in his hair. He looks like a rejected paintbrush from the Crayola factory.

"Caleb is a mess," Luke says, dumping more paint on the baby's tray.

Caleb smiles with his prominent dimples, his green eyes sparkling with mischief.

I take a blob of blue paint and swipe it on Luke's cheek. "There. Now you match."

Luke giggles and wipes his paint-covered fingers on my forehead, all of us consumed by laughter. My heart swells. I've never felt happier than at this moment with my two beautiful boys.

It took me several months to work my way up to the surface, but here I am today, fully present, fully alive, fully me, but improved. I tackled my depression and anxiety with unparalleled vigor. I started by joining moms' groups and getting new friends who could relate to my problems. I incorporated exercise into my routine. I ran and ran, now with a baby jogger. I bought new clothes and made sure to put on makeup every morning, calling it my war paint. Little by little, I found myself again. At night I ravenously read fiction, finding a way to escape mentally. When I find I'm slipping back into the water, I know what to do. I spend some time focusing on me. It takes effort for me to maintain my happiness.

I never got my dream classroom. Losing my career caused me to tumble into a place where I didn't recognize myself anymore, but today I'm fueled by the love I have for my sons. I kick and keep myself on the surface, holding up a raft with my two little boys.

* * *

Other works by Arielle Haughee include "Midnight Mayhem," finalist in Heroes v Villains contest, *Havok Magazine*, July 2016 and "Finding Freedom," *Screamin' Mamas* magazine, summer 2016 issue. She is also featured in the travel blog; *Walk About Florida.*

Visit Arielle's website at: <u>www.ArielleHaughee.com</u>

18

Work in Progress

by Shellie Ambrose-Harms

Current age: 40
Age at the time of loss: 38

Some days I want to attach a sign to myself that says, "Construction zone, pardon my work in progress." One year ago, a transformation process began inside of me that sparked an enthusiasm to have a positive impact on those I connect with in this world, without fatigue or extra pounds.

Being overweight has always been a part of my life. While growing up, I was the tallest in my class and heavier than my classmates. I couldn't share clothes with my friends or match with them. I had to shop in the plus-size section and sometimes dress older than my age. As far back as I can remember, I've always thought that I needed to lose weight, and when I wasn't thinking about it, my family would remind me. Even though I was overweight, it wasn't a dramatic obstacle for me, because I didn't see myself the way mirrors reflected my image. Friendships, athletics, laughter, and romance often distracted me from taking my weight seriously.

Last summer I caught a glimpse of my true reflection, and I did not like what was looking back at me. I felt tired and unmotivated to enjoy the day at the lake. My steps and breaths were labored as I walked the distance from the cottage to the beach. I had to sit down to regroup myself, and dreaded having to walk back up the long trail of stairs. My exhaustion that day caught me by surprise, but I ignored it until I felt it again walking around town. For the first time, my body felt overweight, and I was embarrassed that I couldn't and didn't want to keep up with my friends that day.

My reflection and feelings triggered unwanted emotions. I started researching the easiest way to lose weight. After all, I needed a magical tool to chisel down to the real me I had kept hidden for many years. How I usually felt was joyful, adventurous, energetic, and active. I wanted the world to look at me the way that I felt about myself. Instead, that day at the lake made me wonder if people felt sorry for me or scared for my health. I thought people would choose a label for me that I didn't want to stick to my heart and life. It wasn't that I excitedly accepted being overweight, but up until that day, it didn't hold me back from living life.

I know who I am is not defined by a number on the scale; however, my talents and voice started to become hidden by stereotypes and lack of energy.

Finally in the fall, after a day at Walt Disney World and being asked to get off my favorite ride because the bar wouldn't click down, I acknowledged a sincere need for change.

My birthday adventures led me to a group of people who invited me to a nutrition club. Through their invitation, I lost more than ninety pounds and one hundred inches in less than one year. I made it this far with some assembly required, because of the people in my life. It was much easier than I thought when I found one community that not only helped me succeed, but also celebrated my steps and became some of my closest friends.

I had tried other weight-loss routes, but none gave me results that made me feel unstoppable and healthy. As I was losing weight, I encountered people with a lot of advice and opinions. Someone said to me, "Oh, look, you do have a waist." I always felt like I'd had a waist, so that comment and others like them made me feel like I was clueless about how people viewed me. I eventually learned to listen and apply only the opinions and noise that helped me succeed.

As the weight dropped off, fear increased, because I was worried about what I would look like. Would there be sagging skin? Wrinkles that had been previously hidden? I feared the unknown. At times I sabotaged my success, because I was afraid.

I am still on my weight-loss journey. I have to make daily choices. I have fears to overcome to create a healthy lifestyle for myself and my future. I have more steps to take to reach my goal, but I am not afraid or too exhausted anymore to walk them. I am excited about what is ahead in my life. Dreams that once were stopped or put aside have been reawakened, steps to the lake have been enjoyable, and amusement park rides are repeatedly taken. Loving myself is no longer limited to a dress size or someone's opinion of me.

My steps echoed a realization in my heart that there is a bigger plan for my life than the one that I was living. Each movement toward my goal reminds me that there is a work in me that is determined to be completed.

We need to get out of our own way at times, to experience positive change. There is no easy fix in any area of life, but beautiful moments are often discovered in the construction zones of our lives.

* * *

Visit Shellie's website and blog at:
www.createheartsart.com

19

The Reflection of Loss

by Fern Goodman

Current age: 58
Age at the time of losses: 55 and 57

A re you entitled to a loss if it wasn't yours to lose? I don't mean like almost having the winning lotto numbers and missing out on twenty-five trillion dollars. If you didn't get the job you counted on, that could probably feel like a loss.

What if a person wasn't yours, though, hadn't been in your life for years. Was it your loss?

How about if one loss precipitated another loss that triggered discovery? How many losses does it take to see the light? I declare that if you feel the gut punch of anguish, it's yours to claim.

One of the first friends I met in Vero Beach thirty years ago called me out of the blue. Even though I'd moved away years before, whenever we spoke it was like we were still besties. I was at work but I answered my cell with curious anticipation and a joyful, "Hi ya!"

Bless her; she got right to the point. "I didn't know if you knew or saw the obit, but Jake died Friday night."

Jake? My Jake? (The gut punch) Nonononono. My mind refused to accept the words. It was a mistake; she read it wrong. He was my ex-husband. I still needed him. He symbolized my youth. I had plans for us. Thoughts splintered and zipped around in my head.

"What? No, I didn't know. How did he die?"

"He had lung cancer. My friend Marsha is close to his wife. I'm sorry, I thought you knew."

My chest caved in. I thanked her and hung up. I sucked air into my mouth but was not exhaling. I forced a huge breath out. Over and over I read the obituary she texted me. I had to leave work. My apartment was thankfully connected to my office. To say I broke down would be an understatement. I weaved, bobbed, and crumbled to my knees. My eyes darted frantically for something to grab, to squeeze.

I had no idea he was even ill. Why didn't he tell me? It hurt that he hadn't told me. I could have - what? We hadn't spoken in years. We were both remarried, had our own lives. If I were dying I would have contacted him, I think. I needed to understand, to see him. Facebook! We were friends. I ran to my laptop, knocking over a water bottle on the table. I scanned his photos. He looked pale and thin, eyes sunken. Why hadn't I checked out those photos when he was alive? I would have reached out to him. Damn. Damn. Damn. I had tried to get him to quit smoking. If we had stayed married, would he have quit? Would he still have died? My Jakey. I made him the sweet man he was. He was mine first. How could she let him die on me? On me?

It was more about me than him. I never told anyone that my dream, hope, fantasy, whatever you want to call it, was to end up back with Jake in our golden years. It was a strand of thought, a mantra in the back of my mind. His wife would die before me, and I would be there for him, to comfort him. It would be the cliché reunion. College sweethearts back together after all those years. He was going to be my retirement plan.

He was my only real love. We met at Michigan State. My girlfriends picked him out of the cafeteria lineup and dared me to snag him. The task was easy. He was cute and shy. I caught his attention at the Casino Night event in our dorm. Attendees had to pay for drinks, and as a waitress, I slipped him some freebees and smiled a lot. The trap was set. He asked me out and we fell in love.

I was nineteen and he was twenty when we got married. We lived in married housing on campus during his last year of school. His Irish Catholic mother assumed I was pregnant. Ironically, I never wanted children and Jake did, but we married anyway. He was confident I would change my mind.

During our first year of marriage, my parents retired to Florida. That's when my severe anxiety attacks started. My symptoms ranged from blurred vision to hallucinations. Jake unwaveringly supported me and helped me through my difficult time. When I lay in bed at night shaking violently, he eased his body on top of me and held me tight, to stop the tremors. He never complained or judged me.

He graduated college with an accounting degree and we moved to Florida to get away from the Michigan cold. Jake landed a job with a local CPA firm. We lived with my parents until we had enough money to get an apartment of our own. We soon bought a beautiful home. I never let Jake smoke in the house, hoping he would quit. We went out to breakfast and played cards every Sunday with my parents. We had a great life.

I started working as a travel agent. He was ready to settle down and start a family, while I wanted to travel. We grew in separate ways after five years of marriage. We divorced too hastily.

He had called me once about nine months after the split. My hopes raced when I saw the caller ID. His girlfriend was out of town for a few months, and he wanted to know if I would service him. Yep, would I come over and have meaningless sex? He realized how degrading his request was when he said it out loud, apologized profusely, and hung up. I tried to stay in contact by asking him tax questions until it became awkward. I eventually remarried.

I happened to run into Jake buying beer. He looked terrible, ballooned in weight. My mother had just passed away, and he offered his sympathy. I had expected a card from him, but never received one. That was our only contact in more than twenty years, except for friending each other on Facebook.

After my friend's call, I went to the funeral home website and posted a photograph of Jake when he was young. I wanted to give his family a gift I knew they didn't have. I also wrote an appropriate condolence message inviting the widow to contact me if she wanted to talk about Jake. I never expected or received that call. I will never be able to tell Jake of my dreams for us in our later years. I will always wonder if he ever thought of me, of us.

I went inside my head, reflecting. Life is too short to live unhappy. I questioned everything. He was the sweetest man ever. Why did he have to die before I had another chance with him? I remembered when we were dating, his younger brother had Hodgkin's lymphoma. We visited him in the hospital, and after the visit, Jake cried to me, "Why him, why not me?"

Jake's brother made a full recovery, but that appeal played in my mind. We need to choose our words and life choices carefully. For the previous few years, I'd been too afraid to be by myself, so I stayed in an emotionally abusive marriage. My second husband insulted me, spent all our money, and laid around the house watching television. My light at the end of the tunnel was waiting for Jake to become single, and then I was outta there.

I now had to remap my yellow brick road. Would I rather live alone with an unknown future or stay in a marriage that was like walking through a haunted house? I never knew when the scary monster would pop his head out or stand in my way.

Jake's death compelled me to reevaluate all my relationships. I reconnected with my sister and began collaborating with her on a book. I became more patient with my eighty-nine-year-old father, which deepened our bond. As my writing became more a principle in my life, my husband grew more agitated and angry. Ending a twenty-four-year relationship was a most difficult decision. His job took him away for a month at a time. When I realized I was happier when he was gone, I knew I was finding me again. It was time to act.

My decision began the most difficult sequence of events in my life. My father supported, even encouraged my divorce. In the beginning of July 2015, my father died, and then my divorce became final at the end of the same month.

I'm now without all the men who held a place in my heart. Some days the anxiety of being completely alone is overwhelming. I scanned Jake's Facebook page recently and saw how much he was loved. I wasn't the reason he was smiling in every photo. He found his life mate after he and I divorced. I never loved him enough. The realization and sorrow dropped like a barbell on my core.

One marriage ended too soon; the other lasted too long. Did I make the right decisions? I don't know. What I do know is that one man's demise, who wasn't even in my life at the time, gave me the strength to claim a more gratifying life for myself. I hope I can find that sustainable love. I have moved on, but I'm still working on the letting-go part.

The only theory that helps me through the pain is my belief that everything happens for a reason when the timing is right.

20

Author

by Beda Kantarjian

Current age: 78
Age at the time of loss: 70

I looked at my husband. At seventy-five, he was still the handsome man who once set off a frenzy in 7-11 when mistaken for Sean Connery. He slumped in his usual spot on the couch. He even slept there at night because lying flat had become uncomfortable. The concentrator panted like a dragon, pumping oxygen to his only lung.

"Hey, look at this." The morning paper rustled as he flattened the page. "They're having a Florida Writers Conference in Lake Mary week after next. You have to go," Jerry said.

"Never heard of them." I placed my steaming cup of coffee on the table. "How long does it last?"

"Ummmm, about three days."

"I don't know. This is kind of last minute."

"But your writers group is falling apart. You need to get serious about being a writer. No, author. I'm not gonna call you a writer. You're an author."

What does an author look like, a seventy-year-old grandmother with graying hair and a thickening waist? Could I imagine my picture on the back cover of a book?

If Jerry could, I could.

"With a cheerleader like you, how could I go wrong?" I smiled and shook my head. "But let me learn more about this group, see if they're legit. If they pan out I'll go next year. Okay?"

Although supportive, Jerry also had good instincts when he critiqued my work. Oh, he tread lightly, apologetically, even, when offering criticism, but I insisted he be honest, because he was invariably right.

Even so, I didn't take his suggestion about the conference. I couldn't. Not right then. I felt suspended in time, rooted to the one spot where he and I were always together. If we just stayed very still in place, maybe time wouldn't move. Jerry had not been able to play past nine holes of golf a few weeks before. Prior to that, he had paused only twice for each of his surgeries. It had been nine years since doctors discovered the lung cancer. Statistics predicted fourteen months of life expectancy at that time. He had almost eight bonus years. Good years, celebrating our fiftieth, then fifty-first anniversary, boating with children and grandchildren, celebrating holidays. I thought it would last forever.

A week into the last of his three consecutive hospital stays, I talked with him about his release. The Christmas tree still stood decorated, as it did when I rushed him to the hospital the day after Christmas.

"We'll have a belated New Year's Eve celebration when you get home."

His long, graceful fingers gripped the sheet at his waist. His eyes focused into the distance. "I'm not coming home this time."

"Of course you are. You always come home."

But he didn't.

When beeping from the bedside monitor slowed and then slipped into a piercing, steady wail, its stillness crept into my body. I didn't move. I soaked in Jerry's every feature one more time, from the strong brow bone to his magnificent nose. Somewhere in the space behind me, I was aware of our children rushing from the room. A light touch on my shoulder. My oldest son. I lay my hand on his, and like a drunk, repeated over and over, "I'm half a person." My eyes filled, but didn't overflow.

In the months that followed, I experienced living alone for the first time in my life, but rarely felt alone. More than once at bedtime, the sickening sweet smell of a gift bar of soap I'd forbidden Jerry to use filled the room, weeks after I'd thrown it away. He loved to tease me once in a while by lathering with it.

Jerry had hated green. The color suddenly looked bilious to me. I pitched all my green clothing. Finally I could buy my favorite chunky peanut butter, but it grew stale, half eaten. I replaced it with his smooth brand. Maybe I *was* more than half a person. When new situations came up, I knew exactly how he'd respond. There was no question about the next Florida Writers Association Conference. I would go.

The following October I walked into a cavernous hall filled with strangers at the Marriott in Lake Mary, Florida. The smell of steaming coffee, eggs, and bacon felt welcoming. A low rumble of voices eventually quieted as workers sectioned off smaller spaces with rolling walls.

After the first workshop concluded, a familiar feeling washed over me. It brought me back to a day many years before. At the lunch break of a one-day mini conference in Maitland, I had stepped outside and called Jerry.

"How's it going?" he asked.

My voice shook with excitement. "There's a whole room full of people in there just like me!" That day I felt the same as I did back then, and hoped he knew.

Banquet night a smiling woman sat at a back table with an empty seat nearby. She invited me to join her. It seemed everyone was from another area, and I expected her to be, but Joan lived in Sanford. I invited her to visit my old writing group. She accepted, but though she enjoyed the other writers, our methods weren't a fit for her. Neither did they fit me any longer, I realized.

Two years later we met again at the conference, where she, Bruce, another writer, and I decided it was time to act. Surely there were enough local writers to start a critique group. We held our first meeting at the Lake Mary library on March 14 the following year. Later Bruce's work forced him to drop out of a leadership role, but he remained a member.

Joan and I pinch ourselves often to be sure all that has happened is real. In a little more than four years Seminole

County Writers Group has attracted talented, serious writers dedicated to improving themselves and others in the group. Each year as many as ten of our members' stories are selected for inclusion in FWA Collections, an anthology. Several members have won multiple Royal Palm Literary Awards and have published short stories and novels. We've also become close friends. Who knows you better than one who reads your work?

Yes, I had to start a new, unfamiliar life, but Jerry led me to the start-over point, as an author among authors.

21

To Everything, There is a Season

by Erika Hoffman

Current age: 64
Age at the time of loss: 61

I read the greeting cards. I smell the flowers. I browse the e-mails, kind and concerned. The phone rings. I answer it with a voice so small that it surprises even me. I hear a man say, "Let the memories begin," and I wonder who this person is who begins his condolences this way. The voice continues, "Your family has been selected to receive an all-inclusive..." I hang up after pressing "two" to be removed from the list. I place the receiver back in its cradle. With chin in hand, I glance out the window at the smiling sun and the trees swaying as cars drive past. I think, *The world goes on as if nothing has changed. Yet everything has changed.*

Sometimes I feel silly when I tell folks how old I am and how old Dad was. They look as if they want to ask, "What did you expect?" He'd had a stroke. I knew the odds, yet he seemed to be recovering. He was supposed to be moved from the hospital to rehab at a nursing home. He'd spent ten days in the hospital. Although he had trouble swallowing and I needed to spoon-feed him, his spirits were good. I'd met with the caseworker who found him a bed in a rehab facility. I was adjusting to the next phase of my caregiving. I was pondering the adjustments I'd make to the house when he got released from the care facility. I was thinking about options and whether I'd need to hire someone to stay with him when I couldn't be home. I was preparing myself mentally for the adjustment in parental caregiving. I didn't consider his dying.

I recall long ago when I was young, how sad my father-in-law was when his own father passed at the ripe old age of ninety-six. I recollect how astonished I felt witnessing his grief. I thought about how long a life my hubby's grandpa had lived and what a satisfying life he'd led. I could be very rational about his passing. After all, didn't everyone have to die someday? Back then, young and inexperienced about loss, I looked at my husband's grandpa's death with objectivity.

Now I see it differently. Despite the fact that you are old and despite the fact that your parent has beaten the actuarial odds, your grief is not less. If anything, it is compounded. You've had more years with him to know him through adult eyes or as a buddy. You may have had the experience of caring for your elder in your own home, and he may have seemed like your child then. You have shared simple pleasures with him. If your elderly parent lived with you as my dad did, he is part of your daily routine, and when he's gone, you search for him. You see the dent in the armchair where he sat or the spot on the sofa back where he laid his head or the crossword puzzle lying on the end table not yet finished with pencil posited across it, waiting, waiting for his return. You see his cap and jacket on the hat tree. You see his slippers by his bed, his clothes in the closet. You still have his winter coat to pick up at the dry cleaners. Things look the same, yet all is different, and never will be the same again.

The greeting cards help. The bouquets help. The calls asking you out to lunch help, but you don't want to go. You feel sluggish, not depressed, just sad. You miss his asking you for a glass of water or to help him locate his cane, his asking you to turn on the TV as you watch him fiddle with a remote held upside down in his gnarled hands. You flip on his favorite TV channel. He thanks you and studies you as if you are a technical wizard. You remember all these little things. Your eyes water. You sniffle.

Today you have chores to do but not those banal ones you complained about before. You have the business duties that come with death. They weigh on you as busy work that constantly reminds you of your loss. You hate how you felt aggrieved before because you had to do all the work for your elder and you were confined, and now you think you'd gladly strap on the backpack of caregiving if you could only hear his voice again, see him smile again, and if you could once more say, "Good night, Dad. I'll see you in the morning." You'd hear him say, "Okay, Erika. See you then," and he'd painstakingly mount the stairs.

Tears stream down. Your friends tell you, "You did everything you could. You should have no regrets." No regrets except the big one–that he is gone. You then open your Bible and read Matthew 5:4 KJV, "Blessed are they who mourn: for they shall be comforted." I sit with the book in my lap. I know the words are true. The Bible says there is a season for everything, and I know that also is true and a season will come when I can once again laugh, remembering Dad's stories and jokes. When I remember then, his presence will be there for me, but now my lips turn downward. I feel a heavy heart, and my shoulders sag.

God gave my dad a peaceful death with me by his side holding his hand. Dad got the death he deserved. God was gentle with him. I thank God for that blessing and for His giving me the kind of father that everyone wants. I am a lucky gal.

22

One Out of Many

by Mary E. McKinstray

Current age: 64
Age at onset: Approximately 56

Rheumatoid arthritis (RA) is an insidious autoimmune disease that destroys the lining of the joints, leading to joint destruction and deformity. Chronic inflammation often damages other organs, such as the eyes, lungs, heart, skin, and digestive system while pain, stiffness, and swelling of the joints, along with fatigue, are often debilitating. I know these things because I'd been a pharmaceutical representative with Merck for more than three decades, at one time working for its specialty division selling drugs exclusively for the treatment of "the arthritides."

When my symptoms first began, I knew I had RA and what lay ahead. What I couldn't foresee was that, in a few short years, I would undergo a transformation from someone who was active and walked an hour every day, spending several more hours quilting, moving back and forth between the cutting table and sewing machine, into someone who could barely crawl out of bed in the morning and walk to the kitchen to make a cup of coffee. After bilateral hip replacements, ten hand surgeries, a laminectomy, and three spinal fusions, I walk with a limp and often use a cane.

One leg may be significantly shorter than the other, a known risk of hip arthroplasty. My surgeon suspects changes in my spinal column, including spinal stenosis (narrowing of the spinal column), are to blame and has referred me to a neurosurgeon. Whatever the reason, I have difficulty walking, maintaining my balance, and remaining upright. The walks I once enjoyed past the ponds and fields near our home to watch the herons and other wildlife are no longer practical. This loss fills me with inexplicable melancholy. Even if I had the energy, the possibility of falling and not being able to make it back home prevent me from trying. I don't consider myself old, but I walk and feel like someone who is utterly ancient.

Not long ago, I lost my balance while doing the simplest thing, bending over to pick up a package left on the front door mat by our letter carrier. I fell outward from the doorway onto the brick patio, realizing right away that my arm was broken and getting up would not be easy. I couldn't push up with one good arm and there was nothing within reach that I could use to pull myself up. My first concern was that our two little dogs and two cats would rush out the door. Even if I'd been on my feet, I'd never be able to catch Lily, our little French Coton. To my amazement, all four were sitting in a row just inside the open doorway, absolutely still, and staring at me with wide eyes. This behavior was entirely new to them. I couldn't help laughing. The yipping and initial excitement that comes with the possibility of company had come to an abrupt halt. As is his custom, the letter carrier rang the doorbell after leaving a package, but he was long gone by the time I'd gotten to the door. With no help in sight and unable to get on my hands and knees, I crawled back inside the house on my stomach to the first available piece of furniture. The fracture was not simple; it never is, and required surgical repair and more metal. A year later my wrist is stiff and achy, and the weight of a small bag of groceries is almost too much to bear.

Another fall outside the post office during a torrential downpour was more embarrassing than painful. As people rushed past, unwilling to help, I was left to crawl to my car where I was able to reach the door handle and pull myself up and into the seat. Completely soaked and dirty from rolling around on the pavement, I was otherwise all right.

On the outside, I suppose I appear perfectly able-bodied. I have become dependent on my cane because it provides more than just physical support; it signals to others that I need a little extra time crossing the road or walking into a store. Perhaps it will prevent someone from running me down, stepping on my heels on my way into a store, or glaring at me when I park in a handicap space.

Metal, tiers of which support my spinal column, replace my hips, and stabilize my wrist and ankle, are invisible. Upon seeing my cane, a few kind strangers have offered to return my shopping cart, something that embarrasses me, for some reason. I suppose it makes me feel vulnerable and old.

When the symptoms first began, I scheduled an appointment with my internist. He confirmed my diagnosis and referred me to a rheumatologist, who prescribed prednisone, a synthetic corticosteroid that is an anti-inflammatory and immunosuppressant, Plaquenil, an anti-malarial, and injected the occasional swollen, painful joint with more steroids. A year later I was no better and knew that I was never going to be, if I continued down the same path. Long-term prednisone use can cause weight gain and other unpleasant side effects. It can also lead to osteoporosis (brittle bones), which I now have and for which I receive injections twice yearly. During my final visit to the same rheumatologist, newly returned from vacation, he complained to me that he'd had to sit next to fatties on the airplane. Acutely aware of the weight I'd gained on prednisone, I was mortified. I never went back to him, and instead began searching for a new physician.

She initiated an aggressive treatment plan that included a biologic in addition to the previous drugs. These newer biologics work by impairing the immune system, thereby controlling inflammation. Remission is a possibility with these drugs, but they do not come without risk. Because of their effect on the immune system, they leave you vulnerable to infection. Frequent bouts of respiratory and urinary tract infections have added two more specialties, urology and pulmonary to my repertoire. No sooner is one infection cleared than another presents. More potent antibiotics are necessary for longer periods of time. The cycle is never-ending.

Testing for tuberculosis is required before starting therapy with a biologic. After the first biologic failed and before starting the second, my physician retested me for TB. When the results came back positive, I was stunned. With my immune system weakened, I'd apparently contracted TB somewhere along the line, so I was referred to yet another specialist, one who worked with infectious diseases.

For the next six weeks I was in a state of limbo waiting to be seen by a specialist and all the while thinking that this time I would be on antibiotics for the better part of a year. It also meant that I wouldn't be able to start the new biologic. Instead I went back on prednisone for the unremitting joint pain. In a turn of events, I was thankful to learn that false positives are not uncommon with the QuantiFERON TB test. Retesting with an old-fashioned skin-prick test came back negative for TB, and I was able to begin weekly self-injections of the new drug.

Another change in therapy involved an IV infusion of a chemotherapy drug often used in the treatment of rheumatoid arthritis. Afterward I suffered a grand mal seizure and woke in the ER, where I suffered a second seizure. The months that followed were lost to me. Gone. I had difficulty retrieving words and speaking, and my family was deeply concerned when I couldn't remember recent events.

Last week I had a follow-up electroencephalogram. According to the neurologist, the last one was grossly abnormal, and he is considering adding another anti-seizure medication.

Because depression often accompanies a chronic, debilitating illness, my internist prescribed an antidepressant. I've sold those drugs too, and I have chosen not to add one more drug to my growing list of medications.

For the past several months I've had difficulty breathing, along with a persistent dry cough and excruciating rib pain with every cough. I thought it was another respiratory infection that had progressed to pneumonia. In the ER and in respiratory distress, I was given more prednisone.

Yesterday I spent much of the day in the hospital being seen by a pulmonologist and undergoing laboratory tests and a high resolution x-ray computed tomography (CT) scan. The pulmonary specialist said he was obligated to run those tests because of the effect RA can have on the lungs. Pleural effusion, a build-up of fluid between the lungs and chest wall; interstitial lung disease, inflammation and scarring of the lungs; pulmonary nodules, growths in the lungs; and bronchiectasis, damage to the airways, can be manifestations of rheumatoid arthritis. Interstitial lung disease (ILD) is difficult to treat and has a high mortality rate. Once diagnosed, the survival rate in patients with RA is 2.6 years, according to an article published in *Arthritis and Rheumatism* (2010). Early diagnosis of ILD may ensure that patients are placed on the lung transplant list sooner. I don't know that I have any of these conditions, but am scheduled to return to the pulmonologist next week to discuss the results.

Rheumatoid arthritis is often misunderstood by the general population. When well-known musician Glenn Frey died recently at the age of sixty-seven from complications of rheumatoid arthritis, people were shocked to learn that RA could kill. The complex, debilitating, and sometimes deadly disease affects an estimated 1.3 million Americans.

I have a theory that there are two kinds of people: those who are suffering from a chronic illness and those who are going to, if they live long enough. My approach is to treat everyone with kindness and compassion, because you never know what battles they may be fighting. My story is just one of many.

23

The Gift of Mourning

by Pamela Sullins

Current age: 52
Age at the time of loss: 28

Loss seems to be a consistent, if not a constant, companion. I have found that there is love after loss, there is grace after loss, and there is growth after loss. Yes, there is more loss after loss, but you learn to see it as the teacher it can be, if you are teachable.

Sometimes loss sneaks up on you; death by a thousand paper cuts. All of a sudden you realize you are bleeding to death. Other times, it is quick, massive, and intense.

It took an abrupt loss for me to begin to open my eyes more clearly to my own life. I felt the proverbial slap in the face, the shaking of my shoulders saying, "Wake up!"

I became a widow at the age of twenty-eight. It was a heartbreaking and pivotal loss. I didn't know it at the time, but the depth of my grief began much, much earlier, and the ripple effects would carry me into becoming the woman I am today at fifty-two. There is a lot of ground to cover, but my desire is that by sharing a small portion of my journey, you will find solace and hope, as I found in the sharing of others.

Kevin and I were married December 28, 1982. We first met in high school, my freshman year, his sophomore year. He had just moved to Florida and was in my civics class, since that subject had not been required in Tennessee. We sat near each other and got along, but he later transferred to another local high school. We didn't see each other again until the end of my senior year. He was home from a college in Ohio he was attending on a football scholarship.

We dated briefly over the summer before I left for a six-week trip across Europe as part of a student exchange program. He wrote me letters while I was away. He even called me once at one of the homes where I was staying in Europe, which was not an easy task more than a decade before cell phones and the Internet existed. I was on another continent and he made the effort to stay connected with me.

After I returned home, we saw each other regularly until he returned to Ohio and I left for my freshman year at Florida State. There were more letters, photos, and phone calls and even a flight to Ohio (on my parents' credit card, without their knowledge). We each dated other people, which I believe we both knew but never talked about.

We were married at an early age. Kevin was twenty and I was nineteen. We loved each other as deeply as we knew how, but while considered adults in age, we were still finding our footing. We began our life together full of love and hope, yet there were things in each of our lives that no one else saw and that we didn't fully understand ourselves.

I started nursing school and earned my license as a registered nurse. Kevin completed five years of college and obtained his CPA license. We had good jobs and were on paths to successful careers. We planned to have three children in our close-knit community. We wanted our children to grow up together with our extended family and friends on the beaches of the west coast of Florida enjoying boating, skiing, and fishing. It was a grand time of our lives, and we knew we were blessed. We did start to see however, what I now understand as deep-seated fears and insecurities. They tore at the fabric of our relationship, paper cuts–some of them deep-that preceded the dark, painful road ahead.

Most of our marital issues were tied to Kevin's childhood experiences and my inherent desire to make things better for him and for us.

I was raised in a stable middle-class home. I was the youngest of four daughters. My parents were still together since marrying in 1943. My family has a history of alcoholism on my father's side, and as a result, my father stopped drinking in the late 1950s, more than a decade before I was born.

Kevin's parents divorced when he was young and there were many painful instances of fighting, along with a multi-generational family history of alcoholism and drug abuse on both sides. He was the oldest of three boys and a strong leader in his family, in school, and in his profession. He was also handsome, likeable, and the life of the party.

One of my earliest memories of the fears and insecurities impacting our lives is when I was in nursing school and went to study for an exam with a female married friend at her condo nearby. We were just settling in to study when we heard a banging on the door. It was Kevin, and he was accusing me of being there for the purpose of being unfaithful. He pulled me out into the lawn area in a you're-coming-with-me way. I apologized to my friend, and Kevin and I left.

We had more of these occurrences over the years, woven in between deeply loving and wonderful experiences. It began to shake our foundation for both of us. We loved each other, but we each acted out at times, feeling pressures and a mounting undercurrent of resentment.

Kevin's career advanced and he became the vice president for a national apparel manufacturer. I had gone back to school to obtain a second degree in marketing, and I began working in Tampa, nearly an hour away.

As we approached our ninth anniversary and nearing the end of our twenties, we also began to be concerned that we had not yet started a family. We still held onto our dream, even through the struggles, and were talking through ideas and options to keep us on our intended path, both as a couple, and, we hoped, as parents. We both scheduled medical tests, counseling, and therapy sessions.

Early in 1992, we needed some distance, a break in the storm, to give us the breathing room to work on our relationship. I was seeing a therapist, as was Kevin. In late January I decided to stay with my sister for a few weeks.

Kevin and I met for dinners and for other scheduled periods of time to talk. Friday, February 22 was one of those times.

We went to dinner at one of our favorite restaurants. He seemed off, not fully himself, and it got worse as he drank during dinner. I tried to be conscious of my responses and not make matters worse, but we ended up talking about his drinking. He had stopped drinking for quite a while earlier in our marriage, so I asked him if he would consider not drinking while we are working through things. His answer tears at my heart to this day. "I'm not going to stop drinking".

Even with that response, there was no fighting or drama during dinner. We talked about our plans for the upcoming weekend. He was heading to Gainesville with a few friends and I was going to a cookout with friends on Saturday. He dropped me off at my sister's house after dinner, and we agreed to talk on Sunday.

I called repeatedly on Sunday, but he didn't answer. I left a few messages, assuming he was late getting back into town. When I still had not reached him, I decided to go to our house around 9:00 p.m. but found it dark and empty. I turned on some lights and checked the answering machine that was blinking. There were several messages from his friends on Saturday morning, asking where he was, saying that they were at their meeting spot. They eventually said that they would wait another fifteen minutes, and then were going to go ahead and leave for Gainesville.

I went into the garage to see if his car was there. It was, so I turned on the light. I stood frozen at the door. He was there, in the car with blood on his face. Time stopped. The next thing I remember, I was on the phone and calling 911. I have no idea exactly what I said, other than that my husband appeared to have been shot.

The sheriff's department and EMS showed up quickly. I was taken to the ambulance. I'm not sure if I was sitting alone or with someone. Everything was intense and muted at the same time. Through it all, I felt like I was walking around in a bubble. Words and experiences floated by but didn't take hold.

The police told me that he hadn't been shot and that it appeared to be carbon monoxide poisoning. They wouldn't be sure until the autopsy was completed. I recall a conversation with Kevin's brother, a member of the sheriff's department, but not the time that it occurred. He shared with me that he had heard the dispatch to our address on the radio and was afraid that Kevin may have shot me.

I don't remember how I got to my parents' house or much of anything else. I do remember crying myself to sleep in my mother's arms.

The next day was a mixture of knowing that others needed support, needing to tend to funeral plans, but not wanting to get out of bed. Family and friends stepped in to help, but the only thing that kept running through my mind was, *I should have been there.*

I can't tell you how many times I'd driven us home from a party because Kevin had had too much to drink. He'd pass out in the passenger seat and I'd leave him there to sleep it off in the garage.

In meeting with the funeral home director, we knew it would be a closed casket, because of the state of Kevin's body. Well-meaning people told me I should not bury him with his wedding ring, because it might get stolen, but I wanted it with him, and I chose to trust that it would remain with him.

The funeral was surreal, a blend of tears and laughter, hope and despair. After a short ceremony at the cemetery, I took a rose from the spray and went home with my family.

The autopsy results came back: accidental carbon monoxide poisoning. He was otherwise healthy, and when the coroner spoke with Kevin's therapist, the therapist did not think Kevin was suicidal. As I continued to read the report, I learned that his doctor had put him on Xanax. I had no idea, but it explained some of his recent behavior. I felt anger set in, because I knew what the lethal combination of prescription medications and alcohol had done to his family. I also learned from friends that Kevin had visited a local bar after he dropped me home after our dinner.

Many well-meaning messages swirled around me. "He's in a better place; you should rejoice." "You're still young; you have your whole life ahead of you." "You should move to Tampa and start a new life."

We lived in a relatively small town where we knew many people. I had lived there since I was six and Kevin had made many friends, many wanting to help with my decision-making. "What are you going to do with the house? I know someone who manages estate sales."

I tried to go home and go through our things. I would get through a few things, but then fall into a heap on the floor. I couldn't do it. I just couldn't.

I ended up taking only a few things for myself and invited his family come over to get any items they wanted. I had a stranger go through the rest of the things and either give them away or sell them prior to selling the house. Newly married friends of ours decided to buy our home. A new family and new memories would be made there.

After a week or two, I went back to work. Shortly thereafter, I found a small apartment and moved in with very little. My work friends rallied around me. They were an active, busy group, so it kept me from sitting at home. We went out, we played on a corporate volleyball team, and we competed together in other sporting events.

It was the early 1990s, devoid of helpful books or support groups, particularly specific to a woman my age. I did find a master of social work student counselor through the local university and attended three grief-counseling sessions. I wrote a letter to Kevin, punched some pillows, and thought I was done.

A couple of months later, I bought a townhome, intent on building a new life, but not exactly sure what that life would look like.

* * *

When I originally graduated from high school and went to college, my plan was to major in journalism. I also made the statement at the age of seventeen that I would never marry before the age of twenty-six, which was still my plan when I arrived at college in 1981. I went through rush and pledged a sorority and enjoyed being on a new adventure with high school friends and new friends. I did have challenges—most freshmen do—but I didn't share them. Internalizing them gave way to shame and fear, and I impatiently traded in my dream. I moved back home, married Kevin, and decided on nursing school.

I didn't want to trade in my dreams again. I watched the movie *City Slickers* with some friends, where Billy Crystal stated to his friend who was going through a divorce, "Your life is a do-over." I thought, *Yes, that's right!*

My father was an attorney and a judge, so maybe I would attend law school. I had considered it before. I also thought about taking some extended time off and going to Martha's Vineyard to write and journal. I pondered this thought and many others as I built my network of friends and experiences in my new home and maintained contact with friends and family in my hometown.

I felt as if I was doing well. I had been widowed for a year and I was building a new life. I can see now that I was like a reed floating on the waves. I was becoming adept at adjusting to my surroundings, rather than being rooted in an understanding of who I was as an individual. The busyness of life, while it kept me moving forward, also distracted me from the interior work I needed to go through to grieve fully and to grow. This shortcoming would become apparent over the course of the next few years.

The wave of activity and distractions kept me moving further and further into a new relationship. He was part of the community that surrounded me in Tampa after Kevin's death. A warm and caring man, he had many friends and a deep tie to our community. We married in November 1993 and were part of a small, close-knit group of couples that were also our neighbors.

After a couple of years, we built a new home and moved a few miles away, but kept close ties with our friends. We were as busy as ever with life in general and vacationing with family and friends.

I threw myself into work and excelled. I had a large circle of friends and friends of friends, yet I felt alone, disconnected.

Cracks in my façade started to show. I found grief spilling into my daily life more and more frequently. I once read that the death of a loved one is like an amputation. There are phantom pains that occur without notice.

My new husband would say, "Why can't you just be happy? Why do you have to think and talk about things so much?" He thought my grief meant I didn't love him.

My busy life and our parties became a method of self-medicating that further launched me into what I now know was depression. When I drank, the emotions I kept stuffed inside came out in unhealthy ways. I looked for ways to escape in the moment. I didn't see it at the time, but it was a pattern, like being lame and trying to walk without crutches, limping, falling, a threat of injury to myself and others.

I didn't understand. It had been years since I'd lost Kevin. I had a new life, a new husband, a successful career, friends, travel, and a new home, I knew something had to change, and I was sure that it was me.

My pain took a toll on our marriage, and we divorced. Divorce was in many ways more difficult than the separation caused by death. Death is abrupt and final, there is no going back, no discussion. At least one soul is at peace.

I bought a small house, just big enough for me. I was ready to be on my own for a while. I had begun going back to church and started seeing a therapist and journaling again.

My ex-husband and I had one of our best conversations in months, standing on the steps of the courthouse after our divorce was finalized. We rarely spoke after that day. He was a wonderful man, and I deeply regret the pain that my pain caused him. I am happy that he has found love and a new life.

I began meeting weekly with a small group of women from church. I embarked on a process to inventory my past, my present, and my future. Who am I? What is my passion? I wrote down what I discovered. I had no idea how powerful that process could be.

One of the associate pastors at our church was also divorced and started a Divorce Recovery Workshop. I was two years out from my separation and divorce, so I thought it would be a good thing, even though I thought I was in a good place. I had learned that lesson.

The men and women in the group were at many stages of divorce. Some, like me, were further down the path. Others had spouses leave only a few weeks prior. It was a compassionate, meaningful, and intimate process we shared with each other.

One man in the group, around my age, was also two years out from his divorce from his wife of ten years. He was a musician and had driven across the country from Los Angeles to Tampa to be near his family.

We ended up having an unexpected date when three of us were going to an art show and my friend canceled at the last minute. We went to dinner and then dessert at a small coffee shop and talked for hours.

I learned that he was an alcoholic (red flag) and had been sober for nine years. His sobriety was encouraging, but the red flag remained. We continued to see each other and we talked a great deal about deep and intimate topics.

At one point he told me, "I love you because of who you are, not what you do."

I was stunned. His comment sparked a conversation that brought us to the realization that we had both been struck by Scott Peck's definition of love, "Love is the will to extend one's self for the purpose of nurturing one's own or another's spiritual growth. Love is as love does. Love is an act of will-namely, both an intention and an action. Will also implies choice. We do not have to love. We choose to love."

I married the musician in May 2000 at the age of thirty-six. Our pastor, who led the Divorce Recovery Group, officiated our wedding and shared, "This is a couple who knows something about resurrection."

The sixteen years of my third marriage have been the most fulfilling of my life. They have not been easy, but they have been beautiful.

Together we've dealt with depression, severe family illnesses and deaths, the attacks of September 11, infertility treatments, career changes leading to more identity work, and losses from the 2007 financial crisis.

The most significant experience was the birth of our daughter in 2005. I felt a shift in the universe the moment I laid eyes on her. The love and encouragement that I have the honor to give and receive is like nothing I could have ever imagined.

I know my husband and I will share more happiness and more sorrow, but I know at my core that I am beloved. I choose to love, and I am loved in return.

I thought the death of my husband twenty-four years ago would be *The* loss. *How could there be others?* Now I know otherwise.

I had expectations, which is a risky endeavor itself, but mine were also unrealistic. I now accept that sorrow and suffering can be the companions to peace and joy. I still dream, but I now know that if or when those dreams are lost, they can be re-imagined, as long as I stay patient and open.

I close with a quote by Anne Morrow Lindbergh in *Gift From the Sea*, "Perhaps this is the most important thing for me to take back from beach living: simply the memory that each cycle of the tide is valid; each cycle of the wave is valid; each cycle of a relationship is valid."

Conclusion

Follow-up to
Wife of the Deceased

by Dawn M. Bell

Current age: 45
Age at time of loss: 39

M any people have asked me "What's happened since the book ended?" or "When will you publish Part Two?"

My response was "I'm not sure I'll write in the same genre." While inside my reaction was an incredulous, *Ahhhh, never. I'm done sharing my diary.* I based my reaction on how difficult it was to write the memoir and because of the extreme level of exposure I felt once I published it. The exposure was something I could not have prepared myself for. I still feel it today, but on a much lesser scale.

I wove three and a half years of my journal entries into *Wife of the Deceased.* I began with the day of Matt's death on September 3, 2010, and ended on February 26, 2014, the day I finished the memoir. I'm adding this conclusion as a follow up to the memoir because a few things surrounding grief have surprised me in the last couple years.

My memoir ended in February 2014, when Ava and I had just closed on our new condo we planned to move into in June. I turned forty-three at the end of the month and Ava turned eight at the end of March. I spent most of April and May packing the house into boxes and staging them in the garage along with most of our furniture.

I brought Ava into her toy room to divide things into three piles: keep, pass on to cousins, or donate. It seemed everything was in the keep pile, until I informed Ava that she was tasked with packing what she wanted to keep. Suddenly her generosity knew no bounds, and she kept only enough toys to fill a couple boxes.

My hardest part was going through Matt's personal drawers, his side of the bathroom, and the things he'd stored in the garage. I'd been happily ignoring those areas but was forced to face them. I kept many of his things, but I sent his grandfather's train set and pocketknife, along with his father's watch, to Matt's family. I sent two of his own watches, plane models, and other things to the close friends he'd met in flight school. I sent one of his two flight jackets to a teenage boy with whom Matt felt a bond. It was not hard to choose who would receive each personal item. As soon as I came across an object, the name of the person it should be sent to popped into my head as though it were being spoken to me. I felt Matt was with me that day, helping me.

Once I'd finished boxing all his things, I burst into tears. It was an intense cry that ended as quickly as it started. I liken it to standing in a soundproof room, opening the door and being immersed in incredibly loud music, and then shutting the door and returning to absolute silence.

Summer 2014, almost four years after Matt's death

I thought it would be hard to move out of the house, the house Matt had bought for our family and the last home he had been alive in. It wasn't. I was ready to move, and I knew he'd be with us, not with the house.

When the house was empty, I came back one last time for a slow walk through. I lingered in each room and pictured him where he would likely have been had I just walked in. I was flooded with many wonderful memories. I thought I'd weep, maybe even just a solitary tear, but I didn't.

I walked out and never looked back. I still own the home and rent it to wonderful tenants, but I've never walked back in, and I know I never will. While I don't want to live there again, I want my memory of the home as it was to be sealed in my mind forever. I can't bear the thought of seeing another family's possessions where ours had once been.

I was surprised that it was actually much harder to move into our new home versus leaving the old home. I knew Matt would've loved the new condo and its location. It saddened me that he would never be a part of this new chapter.

Father's Day was June 15 that year. Ava and I were in church listening to the sermon. The pastor asked members of the congregation, if they were willing, to raise their hands if they'd lost their fathers. Ava raised her hand, and we heard someone behind us gasp. I can't be sure it was because my eight-year-old's hand was raised, but I believe it was. When I scanned the sanctuary, the only other hands I saw in the air belonged to people my age and older.

I squeezed her knee and gave her a quick smile. I was proud of her and also relieved by her strength. Certain things made her saddened by her loss, but for the most part, she held her chin up and thought of her father's passing as a part of her life.

In July we traveled to Memphis to attend my dear friend Amy's wedding. It was the first wedding I had attended since Matt's passing, and I was grumpy all week leading up to the trip. If Amy were not so special to me, I wouldn't have gone.

In the crowded concourse while Ava and I waited for the plane to begin boarding, I scored one empty seat at the end of a row. Ava sat, while I stood by her and our luggage. I was focusing on the flight monitors when I heard a question directed at me from the gentleman sitting to Ava's left. "Would you like to sit by your daughter?"

"No, thank you. I've been sitting all morning. I'd rather stand," I replied tersely. In truth I was too wound up to sit. I'd been struggling to keep Ava off the nasty floor for fifteen minutes, and I was irritated at having decided to go to the wedding, and even more frustrated because I couldn't figure out why. *Was I jealous? No. I wasn't interested in being remarried yet. Did I wish Matt were with me? Sure, but I wished that all the time.* I supposed I was dreading the joy and celebration of a couple joining together while my marriage ended painfully and abruptly. I didn't feel like sitting and I didn't feel like talking.

The gentleman asked me a couple of questions, though, and we started a conversation. He was charismatic and easy to talk to. I found myself relaxing and enjoying the exchange. It's a longer story than can be written here, but he shared what had brought him to this area and how he had met his current wife. It was a beautiful story and one I found quite personal. I was curious why he shared it voluntarily. I told him nothing about me other than we were going to a friend's wedding. His words held an important message and gave me a different perspective with which to approach the weekend. That person out of nowhere aided me greatly, and I don't believe it was a coincidence or a random event.

* * *

In August someone brought to my attention that I wasn't disciplining Ava effectively. These too were a stranger's words. They cut like a knife, but I knew they were true. I doubt my conversation with that person was a coincidence either.

I knew I hadn't been disciplining Ava because I felt sorry for her because her father died. She was becoming quite sassy and disrespectful toward me, but I put up with it. I recalled close friends and family members correcting her behavior over the past few months. Many times I'd overheard, "You shouldn't speak to your mother like that."

My behavior was the opposite of how I had been parenting Ava shortly after Matt passed. Back then everything in my life fell out of control. I didn't have the energy or frame of mind to discipline her correctly, so I chose the easiest way to keep her in line, and I had been overly stern with her.

I took the stranger's advice and buckled down. Ava didn't receive the change well, when I transitioned from the lax mom to the mom who stepped up to her job. Ava made it clear she preferred it the other way around, but after a few bumpy months, we worked it out.

Fall 2014, four-year anniversary of Matt's death

The four-year anniversary arrived on September 3. The week prior was difficult and filled with trepidation. I experienced a roller coaster of emotions throughout the day but thankfully never fell into depression. I was concerned that I might plunge emotionally, because I'd been reading my memoir numerous times over the previous four months for initial and final editing, print, and e-book formatting. I wasn't in a good place mentally.

I would read the woman's story and feel so sorry for her, but that woman was me. Years had passed since I'd written the words in my journal the first time, and months had passed since I'd finished the memoir. My memory had blurred over the extreme details of the loss, unlike what I had written in my journal and later transcribed into my memoir. I was removed from the story, even though I had written it and was the main character. It's disconcerting to "visit" yourself at the lowest points in your life and remember what a mess you had been.

Being enveloped in the book over the past few months affected my appearance and emotional health. Sometime in mid-September I was told I looked like I was wasting away. *Wonderful...thanks a lot.* Once again I felt if I'd gained weight rather than lost it, not a word would've been said.

* * *

Later in the month I upgraded my iPhone. That evening Ava and I were meeting friends for dinner. As we sat in the car waiting for them to arrive, I decided to sync the new phone to the Bluetooth in my SUV. I followed the steps and was instructed to record my voice and device. I spoke, "Dawn's cell phone." The Bluetooth system could recognize up to three devices at one time, but only one could connect. When a device was brought in to the vehicle, the system would announce which device connected by playing the voice recording. Therefore, every time I started the SUV and had my cell with me, I heard my recorded voice through the speakers saying, "Dawn's cell phone."

I finished syncing my new phone and was prompted to delete unused devices. Without thinking I pushed the button to continue, and out of the speakers came Matt's voice, "Matt Bell's cell phone." I stopped breathing. I felt a thick, cold fog charged with static fill the SUV.

I heard Ava's little voice from the back seat, "Was that Daddy?"

"Yeah, ummm," I stuttered, "I-I'm sorry, I didn't know..."

"No, that's all right," she spoke over me just above a whisper. "I like to hear his voice."

"Yeah. Me too."

* * *

I held my book signing and launch on October 4 in the event area at the back of a nearby restaurant. My friend Leslie had issued a press release that announced the event. The preceding week was exciting, and I had to pinch myself every day to make sure the launch was really happening. I received many kind messages in the days surrounding the book signing. Friends and family sent beautiful floral arrangements, cookies decorated with my book cover, chocolate bars with my book cover printed on the wrapper, and other gifts to my home and the venue. *Thank you, Leslie, Nancy, Rich, Kristen, Alicia, Amy, Jay, Sarah, Elaine, Bill, Katy, Melanie, Gina, and Trista.*

My dear friend Michelle and her daughter drove down from Atlanta to help with the event. I couldn't have done it without her. Close to one hundred people attended, and I sold a lot of books. I checked off a major bucket list item that day by launching a book I wrote and published.

Ava and her friends Cecilia and Olivia staffed the attendance book and handed out raffle tickets. We held hourly drawings for free copies of the book. Some of the guests asked Ava to sign her name next to mine. I will never forget the pure joy on her face as she signed. It was a perfect day.

Once the book was available, the feedback poured in. One of my favorite responses was that my story prompted a woman and her husband to get their wills written. Another favorite was a man who said he would now be more attentive to his wife.

Many readers were surprised by the duration of our grief. Our culture appears to unconsciously assign a grief time frame for different types of loss. The death of a spouse nets six months to a year. I was under the same belief until it happened to me. The first year was definitely the hardest, but waves of grief continued to hit me, even four years later. I have reached the deep depth of despair a number of times, but the duration is never as long as what I suffered repeatedly in the first year. I learned that if I faced the pain head-on instead of railing against it or burying it, my coping skills increased. I became more adept at crawling out of depression.

Many readers were unsettled by the amount of grief Ava endured, considering she was only four at the time of Matt's accident. A common reaction was that perhaps children aren't as resilient as was believed. I was very pleased to read reactions such as that one and hoped that it might alter the conventional way of thinking. I've never agreed with the phrase 'children are resilient'.

I have learned in counseling that children appear resilient because they're not reacting as an adult would, but how can they? Quite often when children experience a great tragedy, or neglect, they cannot express their feelings because they don't have a reference for the level of suffering, or they don't know how to identify the emotions they are feeling, so they appear not to react at all. If questioned they clam up or give a simple answer. Their behavior doesn't mean they're resilient. It means they can't express their feelings and they're likely burying their pain. Unfortunately that pain will likely surface at some point later in life, and they won't even know what's causing it.

Some friends contacted me with an apology for not doing more for my daughter and me saying, "I didn't know it was that bad." Of course they didn't know. How could they know? I certainly wasn't telling them.

Unless you've experienced a devastating loss, you can't possibly know the overwhelming pain and sadness of the griever. I tried very hard to convey that point in my memoir. If you read it, you will have a glimpse of one person's walk through grief. My hope is that it will help you in your own time of loss or prepare you to help someone else.

I can say with complete honesty there is not one person I feel could have or should have helped me more than he or she did. I am nothing but grateful for the tremendous amount of love and support we did receive. I trust that everyone did as much as they were capable of doing. And for the friends and family who worried they'd said the wrong thing to me as I grieved, this quote is for you:

> The friend who holds your hand
> and says the wrong thing
> is made of dearer stuff than
> the one who stays away.
> —Barbara Kingsolver

Spring 2015, about four and a half years after Matt's death

Ava was reflective over these two months. She was especially attentive to me and overly appreciative for things I did for her. That Easter she spent almost all of her birthday money buying gifts for me. I thanked her and added that she should have bought things for herself. She replied, "I know, but I didn't want to."

One day we were in the car with Ava's friend, who was telling us about her upcoming birthday party. She said her dad wouldn't be there because he'd be out of town the day of her party. Ava responded thoughtfully, "Now you know how I feel."

Another day Ava had returned from a play date and mentioned how strict the girl's parent had been. We were sitting near each other on the sofa. Jokingly I said, "Hmmmm, maybe I should be more strict."

Ava leaned into me and said softly, "No, don't ever be like that. You're all I've got."

That spring was notable for me as well. One evening I was having dinner with a friend that I hadn't seen for a couple months. We were catching up on what had been going on with each of us. I started talking about the highlights of my spring and found that each story involved me being unlike I'd been for years. It seemed I'd been unrestricted and bold and flirtatious. I'd had so much fun. I kept saying, "I don't know what got into me that night."

Not until I was in bed later did I recount the conversation. I put it together and came to an astounding realization. *I'm through grieving.* My actions over the previous couple of months weren't unlike me; they were only unlike me since Matt had passed. The happy-go-lucky, ready-to-have-fun behavior was very much like me the majority of my life. It had just been dormant. I understand now and can say without a sliver of doubt that it took me four years and seven months to grieve the loss of my husband. It was not until this time that I felt truly ready and interested in the possibility of welcoming a new man into my life.

I will always hold some level of grief for the loss of my husband, but the longing and desire to love only him and be partnered with only him was gone.

September 3, 2015, the five-year anniversary of Matt's death

I didn't sleep well the night before and was feeling a bit numb. The same morning five years prior, I had dropped Ava at pre-K, raced to a doctor's appointment, and then hung out at Starbucks and worked a crossword puzzle, waiting for the mall to open. A few hours later Matt's airplane crash-landed.

This morning I had an appointment with the same doctor I'd seen the morning of Matt's accident. It had originally been set for the week prior, because I thought it was too eerie to repeat the same appointment exactly five years later, but the office had called to reschedule because the doctor had been ill.

"The only appointment we have next week is the morning of September 3."

Seriously? I paused. "I'll take it."

I dropped Ava at school and had an hour and a half before the appointment. The drive would take about twenty-five minutes. As I drove I began to feel-I don't know-stronger, maybe. Perhaps resolute is a better word. Yes, I felt determined.

I decided to go to the same Starbucks to pass the extra hour. I didn't have a crossword puzzle, but I did have a magazine. I ordered coffee and sat. I was careful to assess my emotions. I didn't want to bring undue pain to myself or fall apart.

I was fine.

I looked around and remembered where I'd sat in a lounge chair five years before. The configuration of the coffee shop had changed and there was now a table there, but I knew where I'd been. I let the events of the morning five years prior wash through me.

I next went to my doctor's appointment.

I was still okay.

I exited the parking lot and had a feeling of finality, of something coming full circle. *It's done.* This was my declaration of, "I won't be beat" and a figurative middle finger to September 3.

Only then did I feel the intense weight resulting from the repetition of the two mornings. A few tears rolled down my face. I shook my head at the loss of a great man.

I turned onto 14 to travel the ten miles to my new exit since our move roughly a year before. I employed my strongest coping mechanism, gratitude, and pondered God's blessings in my life. I had an amazing little girl, excellent health, a family who loved us, and great friends, old and new. With each mile the sadness drained out of me like a tower of water being emptied until there was nothing left.

* * *

Today? Today I'm approaching the sixth anniversary of Matt's death. I can honestly report that I am happy and gratefully at peace.

Ava is doing well too. She had a setback last fall that resulted in some regressive behavior, but we reached out for assistance, and she's back on track.

A newer friend, Carolyn, stated recently, "Honoring memories of loved ones while moving on with our own lives is the greatest challenge." I couldn't agree more. Sometimes I still wonder why Matt was taken so young, but those thoughts are no longer fettered with anger and resentment. I just wonder. I trust that some day I will know why. Until then, I work each day to focus on the good, because I know more bad days and sad things will come.

* * *

I hope the stories in this book have served as a reminder that we never know what someone else is going through or what they've endured. I've often thought how helpful it would be if I could know a person's trials just by looking at them. It'd be much easier to turn the other cheek if I were treated unkindly.

I think of the dress uniform I wore in the military. Each ribbon, medal, award, and decoration was outwardly displayed and it told the history of my service. With a quick glance at my uniform, any soldier could identify my rank, years of service, and personal accomplishments. Imagine the power of being able to glance at a person on

the sidewalk and know the pain they've suffered. 𝖢^
the compassion and kindness that would be extended.

Unfortunately we can't know the path another has walked with a quick glance at them. But we can give them the benefit of the doubt.

WIFE OF THE DECEASED

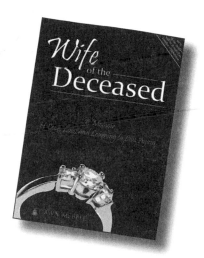

Wife of the Deceased is a personal memoir that spans the three years following the tragic and unexpected death of my husband, Matthew Bell, at thirty-eight years of age. The content is drawn from my journal entries depicting every aspect of my journey through the grieving process. This account of the physical, mental, and emotional effects of grief I experienced following his death is raw and uncensored.

My goal in writing *Wife of the Deceased* is first to honor my husband and the man he was. Secondly, I hope to help anyone in a similar situation by sharing my account of the stages of grief; the extreme rage I felt, the seemingly insane thoughts that went through my head on a day-to-day basis, and the physical assault my body suffered. My goal is to attest to and validate what grievers are feeling and perhaps ease a fraction of the pain and anguish they are living with every day.

Paperback and eBook versions can be purchased at Barnes & Noble and on Amazon.

For signed copies, please contact Dawn at www.DawnMBell.com